Collective Perspectives on Issues Affecting Learning Disabilities

Position Papers, Statements, and Reports

Second Edition

National Joint Committee on Learning Disabilities

© 2001, 1994 by the National Joint Committee on Learning Disabilities

All right reserved. No part of the material protected by this copyright notice may be reproduced or utilized in any form or by any means, electronic or mechanical, including photocopying, recording, or by any information storage and retrieval system, without the prior written permission of the copyright owner.

NOTICE: The copyright holder grants permission to the user of this material to make unlimited copies of this publication for teaching or clinical purposes. Duplication of this material for commercial use is prohibited.

To obtain additional copies of this publication, contact PRO-ED, Inc. 8700 Shoal Creek Boulevard, Austin, TX 78757-6897, 800/897-3202

Library of Congress Cataloging-in-Publication Data

Collective perspectives on issues affecting learning disabilities : position papers statements / National Joint Committee on Learning Disabilities.—2nd ed.
    p.   cm.
  ISBN 0-89079-845-1
    1. Learning disabilities—United States. 2. Learning disabled children—Education—United States. 3. Learning disabled—Services for—United States. 4. Education and state—United States. I. National Joint Committee on Learning Disabilities (U.S.)
LC4705.C65   2000
371.9—dc21
                                                               00--32337
                                                                   CIP

Printed in the United States of America

1 2 3 4 5 6 7 8 9 10   04 03 02 01 00

Contents

Preface • v

Acknowledgments • vii

Overview of the National Joint Committee on Learning Disabilities • 1

- Current Membership • 3
- History of the NJCLD • 5
- Mission Statement • 13
- Operational Procedures • 17

Documents • 23

Basic Issues

- Learning Disabilities: Issues on Definition (1990) • 27
- Learning Disabilities: Issues on Definition (1981) • 33
- Operationalizing the NJCLD Definition of Learning Disabilities for Ongoing Assessment in Schools (1997) • 39
- Issues in Learning Disabilities: Assessment and Diagnosis (1987) • 55
- The Need for Subject Descriptors in Learning Disabilities Research: Preschool Through High School Years (1989) • 63

Professional Development Issues

- Professional Development for Teachers (1999) • 69
- Learning Disabilities: Use of Paraprofessionals (1998) • 79
- Learning Disabilities: Preservice Preparation of General and Special Education Teachers (1997) • 99

- Learning Disabilities: Issues in the Preparation of Professional Personnel (1982) • 109
- In-service Programs in Learning Disabilities (1981) • 115

Preschool and School Issues

- A Reaction to *Full Inclusion:* A Reaffirmation of the Right of Students with Learning Disabilities to a Continuum of Services (1993) • 123
- Providing Appropriate Education for Students with Learning Disabilities in Regular Education Classrooms (1990) • 127
- Learning Disabilities and the Preschool Child (1985) • 135
- Issues in the Delivery of Services to Individuals with Learning Disabilities (1982) • 147

Transition, Postsecondary, and Adult Issues

- Learning Disabilities: Issues in Higher Education (1999) • 155
- Secondary to Postsecondary Education Transition Planning for Students with Learning Disabilities (1994) • 165
- Adults with Learning Disabilities: A Call to Action (1985) • 173

Policy Issues

- Learning Disabilities and the Americans with Disabilities Act (ADA) (1992) • 185
- School Reform: Opportunities for Excellence and Equity for Individuals with Learning Disabilities—A Special Report (1991) • 193

Preface

THIS PUBLICATION PRESENTS THE RESULTS OF OVER A DECADE of work by the National Joint Committee on Learning Disabilities (NJCLD), a national committee of representatives of organizations committed to the education and welfare of individuals with learning disabilities. The current members of the NJCLD are as follows:

- American Speech-Language-Hearing Association (ASHA)
- Association on Higher Education and Disability (AHEAD)
- Council for Learning Disabilities (CLD)
- Division for Children's Communication Development (DCCD), a division of the Council for Exceptional Children (CEC)
- Division for Learning Disabilities (DLD), a division of the Council for Exceptional Children (CEC)
- International Dyslexia Association (IDA)
- International Reading Association (IRA)
- Learning Disabilities Association of America (LDA)
- National Association of School Psychologists (NASP)
- National Center for Learning Disabilities (NCLD)

Over 350,000 individual constitute the membership of the organizations represented by the NJCLD.

A major purpose of the NJCLD is to provide an interdisciplinary forum to review issues for educational and governmental agencies.

The NJCLD also prepares and disseminates statements to various organizations to clarify issues in the area of learning disabilities.

The member organizations represent many different professions and viewpoints with regard to learning disabilities. As Jules Abrams states in his discussion of the history of the committee (see overview), it is to the credit of the members of the NJCLD, and their diverse parent organizations who have supported the committee, that they have been able to achieve accord and to present these statements in a single voice.

Acknowledgments

THE NATIONAL JOINT COMMITTEE ON LEARNING DISABILITIES (NJCLD) wishes to express its appreciation to the Learning Disabilities Association of America and PRO-ED, Inc., for underwriting the production of the first edition of this monograph. This book is published by PRO-ED, Inc., under a special arrangement with the National Joint Committee on Learning Disabilities (NJCLD). Proceeds derived from the sales of this publication will be used to further the work of the NJCLD.

The committee also wishes to thank Sylvia Richardson for her painstaking initial work in putting this monograph together. Sylvia's longtime involvement with the NJCLD allowed her to piece together much of the historical information contained in the publication.

Overview of the National Joint Committee on Learning Disabilities

THIS SECTION OF THE MONOGRAPH PROVIDES A COMPREHENSIVE overview of the National Joint Committee on Learning Disabilities (NJCLD). The four subsections describe the membership of NJCLD, the history of the committee, the primary objectives that guide the work of the committee, and the procedures used by the committee to accomplish its goal.

A major portion of the last three sections of this overview is an adaptation of an article written by Jules C. Abrams that appeared in the February 1987 issue of the *Journal of Learning Disabilities* (Volume 20, pp. 102–106). It is used here with permission of the publisher.

Current Membership of the NJCLD

American Speech-Language-
 Hearing Association (ASHA)
10801 Rockville Pike
Rockville, MD 20852
301/897-5700; 800/498-2071
Web site: www.asha.org

Council for Learning Disabilities
 (CLD)
P.O. Box 40303
Overland Park, KS 66204
913/492-8775
Web site: www.cldinternational.org

Division for Learning Disabilities
 (DLD)
Council for Exceptional Children
1110 Glebe Road, Suite 300
Arlington, VA 22201-5704
800/224-6830
Web site: www.dldcec.org

International Reading Association
 (IRA)
800 Barkdale Road
P.O. Box 8139
Newark, DE 19714-8139
302/731-1600; 800/336-READ
Web site: www.reading.org

National Association of School
 Psychologists (NASP)
4340 East-West Highway
Suite 402
Bethesda, MD 20814
301/657-0270
Web site: www.naspweb.org

Association for Higher Education
 and Disability (AHEAD)
P.O. Box 21192
Columbus, OH 43221-0192
614/488-4972
Web site: www.ahead.org

Division for Children's
 Communication Development
 (DCCD)
Council for Exceptional Children
1110 Glebe Road, Suite 300
Arlington, VA 22201-5704
800/224-6830

International Dyslexia Association
 (IDA)
Chester Building, Suite 382
8600 LaSalle Road
Baltimore, MD 21286-2044
410/296-0232
Web site: www.interdys.org

Learning Disabilities Association of
 America (LDA)
4165 Library Road
Pittsburgh, PA 15234
412/341-1515
Web site: www.ldanatl.org

National Center for Learning
 Disabilities (NCLD)
381 Park Avenue S., Suite 1401
New York, NY
212/545-9665
Web site: www.ncld.org

History of the NJCLD

IN ONE SENSE THE HISTORY OF THE NJCLD MAY BE TRACED back to the first time an individual experienced a severe learning disorder. While learning disabilities obviously have been with us for a long time, the specific term was not coined until early in the 1960s. Through the '60s there was increased sensitivity to, and awareness of, those youngsters with intense difficulties in learning. It was perhaps inevitable that a number of different professional disciplines would become involved in attempting to understand the nature of learning disabilities, their assessment and diagnosis, and models of remediation and intervention. Too frequently, however, these professionals tended to view the problem through their own windows of specialization. A kind of tunnel vision was employed, and important facets of learning disability were ignored.

By 1970, many professional organizations involved in the education of children had begun to focus some of their attention on the individual with learning disability. Yet there was great fragmentation; many of the organizations had little knowledge of what other professional groups were doing. Worse, emotionally laden issues related to territorial imperatives, interprofessional jealousies, programming, and jurisdiction were beginning to flare up, often to the detriment of the child in need. A number of interdisciplinary meetings were held to resolve some of these problems, but the results were minimal. Increasingly, reading specialists fought with special education teachers, special education teachers fought with speech-language pathologists, and everybody blamed the psychologists!

In 1971, the International Reading Association (IRA) established the Disabled Reader Committee, which later developed into the Disabled Reader Special Interest Group of IRA. As chairman of the Disabled Reader Committee, I, J. Abrams, was charged with establishing greater cooperation among the various professions involved with learning disabilities and the reading specialist. In 1974, as part of the effort to fulfill that charge, a conference was held at Johns Hopkins University to discuss issues of definition, assessment, and remediation of children with learning disabilities. People representing a wide variety of professional disciplines were in attendance, but, to my great chagrin and embarrassment, representatives of the Division for Children with Learning Disabilities (DCLD), of the Council for Exceptional Children (CEC), now the Council for Learning Disabilities (CLD), were unintentionally excluded.

Quite justifiably, Dr. Stephen Larsen of DCLD was annoyed by the exclusion of representatives of his organization from the meeting at Johns Hopkins. As chairman of the Professional Liaison Committee of DCLD, Steve's charge was similar to mine—that is, to bring about some rapprochement among the frequently warring groups. Interestingly enough, Steve had been dealing primarily with the speech–language pathologists; he had basically ignored, or at least temporarily put aside, the reading group. So we had the strange, though unfortunately not uncommon, situation where two professional groups, both interested in learning disabilities, were trying to accomplish the very same objectives and were hardly talking to one another.

Steve's angry call to me about DCLD's exclusion from the Johns Hopkins conference set the stage for the development of the Joint Committee on Learning Disabilities (JCLD). The major impetus, of course, was the need to establish greater cooperation among those organizations primarily concerned with individuals with learning disabilities. Steve's previous work with the speech and language groups led almost immediately to the American Speech-Language-Hearing Association's joining the JCLD. Within just a few months, three other organizations (the Association for Children with Learning Disabilities [ACLD], the Division for Children with Communication Disorders [DCCD], and the Orton Dyslexia Society [ODS]) had become part of the committee.

The first official meeting of the JCLD was held October 15 and 16, 1975, in Kansas City, Missouri. Stephen Larsen was elected as first chairman, and it was specified that the number of representatives from each organization would be set at three.

It is of considerable interest to report some of the statements that were made in 1975; many of the issues raised then are still quite relevant today. ACLD called for a shift of emphasis from the development of position papers to the development of delivery of services. It also stated the need to establish and define the link between learning disability and juvenile delinquency, including truancy. ASHA spoke of the changing role of the speech–language pathologist; it pointed out that states continued to write new legislation arising from an outdated role definition for the speech–language pathologist. Both the ODS and IRA spoke to the crucial issue of better communication among the many disciplines and professional groups. IRA and DCLD both agreed that the issue of competencies had to be addressed and should be given top priority. Steve Larsen introduced the highly charged issue of who should be considered competent to work with individuals who are learning disabled.

Ultimately, it was the consensus of the group to address three issues: competencies, service delivery models, and sharing of communication. It was emphasized that concern about definition or jurisdiction should be minimized; what was important was to identify the child's needs and the competencies required to deal with those needs. With regard to membership of JCLD, it was felt that other professional disciplines might be involved in the future, but for the moment, membership would be limited to those with a major commitment to children with learning disabilities.

The second formal meeting of JCLD was held at the national CEC convention in Chicago on April 4 and 5, 1976. With the Education for All Handicapped Children Act of 1975 (P.L. 94-142) now in effect, the committee began to address a number of issues related to persons with learning disabilities. Such topics as teacher training, professional standards, research, and definition, had definite bearing on P.L. 94-142. But the regular work of the committee had to be postponed temporarily as JCLD was asked by Frank King, of the then Bureau of Education for the Handicapped in the U.S. Office of Education, to respond in session to some of the proposed regulations for P.L. 94-142 that dealt with specific learning disabilities.

In October 1976, the JCLD, now chaired by Jules Abrams as IRA's representative, met in Philadelphia. Initially, the major item on the agenda had been to prepare a unified statement in response to the first draft of the Concept Paper on Specific Learning Disabilities (Section 5.b, P.L. 94-142). But unity was not destined to be the hallmark of the Philadelphia meeting. Instead, the underlying and persistent conflicts regarding professional turf and territorial imperatives erupted like a volcano that had been dormant too long. Indeed, there were times when I felt like the secretary general of the United Nations!

The major dilemma of the Philadelphia meeting related to the composition of the screening team. The rancor expressed around this issue was merely the tip of the iceberg. Many members of JCLD felt keenly their responsibility to protect the job security of their constituents. No one questioned that a substantial proportion of children with learning disabilities had problems in reading and language, and that instruction in these areas was a major educational challenge. The real question dealt with which disciplines were competent to teach in these areas. Ultimately, four of the representative organizations submitted a report, but it was noteworthy that a minority report was delivered by ACLD and DCLD. Clearly, there was a great deal of work to be done before the members of JCLD were to achieve any semblance of harmony.

A subcommittee was established to prepare a list of competencies for consideration at the next meeting of JCLD in Washington, D.C. in March 1977. The Washington meeting was also important because it was the first time that JCLD put on its "road show." One representative from each parent organization participated in a panel presentation at the ACLD conference on March 11. The title of the presentation was "Learning Disabilities Regulations for Public Law 94-142: Reaction of the Joint Committee on Learning Disabilities." It is again indicative of the emotional climate of the times that I wrote the following to the participants prior to the presentation:

> While I recognize that it would be impossible for this group to present a "united front" at this time, I do hope that the panel discussion will not deteriorate into a series of vituperative attacks upon one another. We all recognize that there is a great deal of disagreement in the Joint Committee; hopefully some of this will be worked out in our meetings prior to this presentation. On the other hand, I would hope that we could present to our general audience the feeling that we are attempting to work together cooperatively despite our basic disagreements.

From a historical perspective, the next 2 years (1978 and 1979) represent a kind of Dark Ages for the Joint Committee on Learning Disabilities. There were no meetings, and there was little interaction. It was not as if the JCLD had been officially terminated, but it certainly seemed to have faded away. I am not certain of the reason for this. Perhaps the crucible had become too hot and needed some time to cool off. Or maybe the members had to "get away" to replenish their emotional resources.

Our continuing saga now focuses on Katharine Butler, whose herculean efforts and perseverance were largely responsible for the revival of the JCLD. On February 14 and 15, 1980, Kay, representing the American Speech-Language-Hearing Association, presided at the JCLD meeting in Orlando, Florida. It was clear that a new spirit suffused the air, a feeling of optimism that these varied groups could actually work together for the benefit of children with learning disabilities. This should not imply that there no longer was controversy or disagreement. Nevertheless, there seemed to be a very active intention on the part of the members of the committee to overcome the old problems and to effect concrete accomplishments.

At this meeting a number of important decisions were made. The committee was now to be known as the National Joint Committee on Learning Disabilities (NJCLD). Emphasis was to be on individuals with learning disabilities, which included children, adolescents, and adults. There was general agreement that each organization represented on the NJCLD make every attempt to maintain the same representatives in order to facilitate the continuity of the committee and its work. A subcommittee was established to review circulated papers and positions of the member groups regarding definitional issues, and to produce a working draft paper regarding definition of specific learning disability versus learning problems for the consideration of NJCLD at its September 1980 meeting. To facilitate the communication and workings of the NJCLD, a steering committee was formally established with one representative from each parent organization. Finally, it was decided that it would be advisable to minimize the influence of any one organization by no longer scheduling the meetings of NJCLD at national conferences. Two meetings a year would be held on a regular basis—one in September and one in January.

The organization had now moved through its infancy and had survived its latency period. It was now ready to navigate the troubled waters of its adolescence with relative ease. Since 1980, two meetings a year (along with a great deal of work in between) have produced a number of important position papers and other accomplishments. In January 1984, the Division for Learning Disabilities of CEC became a new member of NJCLD. In September 1984, the National Association of School Psychologists (NASP) joined the committee. At the same meeting a policy committee was established to formalize some of the guidelines under which we had been operating for many years.

I [Jules Abrams] have purposely discussed the history of NJCLD in considerable detail. It is important to recognize that this group, which today functions so harmoniously, needed to go through a very difficult developmental period. It is to the credit of the members of NJCLD, and the parent organizations who have supported the committee, that they were able to overcome so many of their problems and to bring about considerable rapprochement. In this way the NJCLD continues to fulfill its basic mission on behalf of the individual with learning disability.

The first official minutes of October 1976 listed the following attending organizations and their representatives:

- **Association for Children with Learning Disabilities** (ACLD): Sandy Harrison, Alice Scogin, Eli Tash

- **American Speech-Language-Hearing Association** (ASHA): Anthony Bashir, William Healey, Harold McGrady

- **Division for Children with Communication Disorders** (DCCD), division of **Council for Exceptional Children:** Katharine Butler, Gloria Engnoth, Frank Falk

- **Division for Children with Learning Disabilities** (DCLD), a division of **Council for Exceptional Children:** Steve Larsen, Phyllis Newcomer, Judy Wilson

- **International Reading Association** (IRA): Jules Abrams (Chairman), Walter MacGinitie, Ralph Staiger
- **The Orton Dyslexia Society** (ODS): Dale Bryant, Gilbert Shiffman

In 1982 the DCLD changed its name to the Council for Learning Disabilities (CLD). The Division for Learning Disabilities (DLD) of the Council for Exceptional Children and the National Association of School Psychologists (NASP) joined the NJCLD in 1984. The ACLD became the Learning Disabilities Association of America (LDA) in 1989. The Association for Handicapped Student Service Programs in Post Secondary Education (AHSSPPE) joined in June 1990, changing its name to the Association on Higher Education and Disability (AHEAD) in 1992. The Orton Dyslexia Society (ODS) became the International Dyslexia Association (IDA) in 1997.

The following list comprises those individuals who have represented the organizations that have belonged to the NJCLD from 1976 through 1999. Several professionals have represented more than one organization. All were actively involved in planning the position statements when they were on the committee, although they may not have been representatives on the NJCLD at the time a statement was finished and accepted for publication.

AHEAD: Lydia Block, Loring Brinckerhoff, Christy Lendman

ASHA: Anthony Bashir, William Healey, Harold McGrady, Katharine Butler, Stan Dublinske, Mabel Rice, Rhonda Work, Nickola Nelson, Ann Bird, Ruth Watkins

DCCD: Katharine Butler, Gloria Engnoth, Rhonda Work, Sara Conlon, Claire Maisel, Joel Stark, Joan Maynard, Sister Rita Alice Fitzgerald, Thomas O'Toole, Elizabeth Wiig, Mary Dale Fitzgerald, Candace Bray, Barbara Ehren, Eleonore Krebs, Judy Montgomery

CLD: Phyllis Newcomer, Steve Larsen, Judy Wilson, Donald Hammill, Gaye McNutt, James Leigh, Don Crump, Ann Netick, James Patton, Kay Cessna, Brian Bryant, Debi Gartland

DLD: Jeanette Fleischner, Sister Marie Grant, Cathy Barlow, Jean Lokerson, Elise Blankenship, Candace Bos, Cindy Terry, Harold McGrady, Sharon Vaughn, Esther Minskoff, Donald Deshler, Cheri Hoy, Dan Hallahan, Naomi Zigmond

IDA: Marcia Henry, Gordon Sherman, Harley Tomey III, Nancy Hennessy, Drake Duane, Dorothy Strickland, William Ellis, Mary Lee Enfield, Linda Frank, Anne O'Flanagan, Sylvia Richardson, Anthony Bashir

IRA: Jules Abrams, Patricia Bricklin, Ralph Staiger, Olive Niles, Jack Cassidy, Lee Indrisano, Peggy Ransom, Carolyn Houk, Linda Gambrell, Janet Gaffney, Carol Beers, Barbara Walker, Richard Allington

LDA: Betty Bader, Sandy Harrison, Sylvia Richardson, Jean Petersen, Alice Scogin, Robert Reed, Shari Sowards, Martha Kabbes, Patsy Fordyce, Anne Fleming, Doris Johnson, Lynne Cannon, Helene Gruber, La Nelle Gallagher, Joe Swalwell, Rosa Hagin, Ann Kornblett, Sandra Britt, Steven Russell, Harrison Sylvester

NASP: Kevin Dwyer, Robert Germain, Neil Browning, James Eikeland, Howard Knoff, Patricia Howard, Susan Safranski, Susan Vess, Larry Sullivan

NCLD: Mark Griffin, William Ellis, Claire Wurtzel

The following individuals have been chairs of the NJCLD and are presented in chronological order:

Steve Larsen (DCLD), Jules Abrams (IRA), William Healey (ASHA), Katharine Butler (ASHA), Drake Duane, (ODS), Sylvia Richardson (ACLD), Joel Stark (DCCD), James Leigh (CLD), Jean Fleischner (DLD), Stan Dublinske (ASHA), Sister Marie Grant (DLD), James Patton (CLD), Kevin Dwyer (NASP), Lynne Cannon (LDA), Candace Bos (DLD), Ann Bird (ASHA), Sylvia Richardson (IDA), and Steven Russell (LDA)

Mission Statement

THE NJCLD LISTS AS ITS PURPOSES THE FOLLOWING:

1. To facilitate communication and cooperation among the member organizations

2. To provide an interdisciplinary forum for the review of issues for educational and governmental agencies, and act as a resource committee for those agencies and other interested groups

3. To provide a response to national issues in the area of learning disabilities when and as the need arises

4. To seek agreement on major issues and problems pertinent to the area of learning disabilities

5. To prepare and disseminate statements to various groups in order to clarify issues in the area of learning disabilities

6. To identify research and service delivery needs in the area of learning disabilities

To a very large extent, the major way in which NJCLD has attempted to achieve these purposes is the preparation and dissemination of its position papers. As is demonstrated in the next section of this paper, the procedures used to write the position papers provide the greatest opportunity to facilitate communication and cooperation among the member organizations. Ideas are gathered, exchanged, deliberated over, fought about, modified, revised, and sometimes compromised in the effort to establish concepts that will be acceptable to all the organizations.

Consonant with its desire to provide an interdisciplinary forum for the review of issues, the NJCLD periodically presents at national conferences of the member organizations. Significant issues that have previously been explored at the NJCLD meetings usually constitute the content of these presentations. It is hoped that members of the various professional organizations can in this way become more familiar with the conceptual position of other groups that work in the area of learning disabilities. Through mutual interaction and discussion, irreconcilable differences frequently prove otherwise; one organization develops a kind of working alliance with another. Ultimately, NJCLD's presentations at national conferences of the various member organizations help "bring about agreement on major issues/problems pertinent to the area of learning disabilities."

The NJCLD always stands ready to provide a response to national issues in the area of learning disabilities when and as the need arises. Particularly in dealing with educational and governmental agencies, the important contribution of the NJCLD is that its reaction represents the unified feeling of a number of different disciplines. Most recently the NJCLD has worked with the Office of Special Education and Rehabilitative Services as well as the Rehabilitation Services Administration.

From its inception, the major objective of the NJCLD has been to develop greater cooperation and understanding among all the professional organizations involved with learning disabilities. At the meetings of the NJCLD, in the frequently exciting and occasionally vituperative discussions that occur, members begin to develop a kind of therapeutic relationship. It is as if the mutual exchange of ideas begins to allow one individual to stand in the shoes of another. And occasionally what evolves is more than just a concordance of ideas. At times, there is a creative leap, as if the group has come together in a remarkable way to innovate as well as to integrate.

Operational Procedures

NO ORGANIZATION AS DIVERSE IN ITS MEMBERSHIP AS THE NJCLD could possibly hope to attain its goals without developing some procedural rules. (During the first few meetings it seemed as if the major component in the process was who could yell the loudest or speak the longest. Oh yes, there were alliances, but they were not therapeutic!) Over the years procedures evolved, modified at times to fit the changing circumstances. As pointed out, certain informal steps were followed until the policy committee was established in 1984 to review the extant guidelines and to formalize them. The process that is delineated is the one developed by the policy committee and approved by the NJCLD. Reference to previous procedures will be made only when important.

One of the very first problems the NJCLD faced had to do with the constituency of the organization. Given its commitment to an interdisciplinary focus, the committee was reluctant to exclude any organization that expressed interest in joining. And despite its relative lack of visibility, a surprisingly large number of groups wanted to join the NJCLD as early as 1976. This posed a real dilemma for the committee. It was not consonant with our professed goals to discourage any organization from joining; on the other hand, it was important to keep the committee sufficiently small so that it could be productive. Initially, it was decided that only those professional organizations or divisions of organizations with a primary interest in learning disabilities would be eligible. In February 1985, the NJCLD approved the following membership requirements:

An organization desiring membership in the NJCLD shall

1. represent a nationally based group;
2. be committed, as a major purpose of its group, to the education and welfare of persons with learning disabilities; or
3. have a structured subgroup that focuses on persons with learning disabilities.

An organization requesting membership in the NJCLD shall

1. submit a letter of interest to the NJCLD chairman;
2. indicate its total members by categories (e.g., regular, associate, student, etc.);
3. describe its specific areas of interest and expertise in learning disabilities;
4. submit its constitution and bylaws with the letter of interest; and

5. upon invitation from the NJCLD, send representatives as observers to at least one NJCLD meeting prior to formal vote on membership.

The NJCLD shall

1. review the requesting organization's letter of interest with accompanying material;

2. invite representatives of that organization to observe at least one NJCLD meeting;

3. approve membership of the requesting organization by a two-thirds majority vote of the NJCLD member organization; each organization shall have a single vote; and

4. inform applicant organization of the status of its request for membership.

When the NJCLD was first established, the chairmanship was rotated annually through the respective organizations. In the beginning this was extremely important, given the political and emotional climate of the times. In a way, the rotation spoke to the paranoid element that pervaded the thinking during those early years. No one organization could have the opportunity to exert too much influence on the NJCLD. Over the years, as mentioned previously, suspicion became minimal, rancor subsided, and people could relate to one another, rather than from group to group. Currently the official statement of the NJCLD regarding its chairman reads as follows:

The Chairman of the NJCLD shall be elected annually at the fall meeting by a majority vote of the representatives. The chairman shall serve a one-year term beginning in January of each year and may serve two consecutive terms. The chairman must have been a representative in attendance at the NJCLD for a minimum of twelve (12) months preceding his/her election.

The duties of the chairman shall include, but not be limited to, the following:

1. Presiding at all meetings of the NJCLD

2. Preparing an agenda for each meeting and circulating it to all members prior to the meeting

3. Notifying members of the time and place of each meeting

4. Appointing a secretary

The most tangible evidence of NJCLD's accomplishments is its position papers, so I will describe in some detail how these are written. The process begins when the NJCLD at one of its annual meetings chooses a particular area or sphere of interest to investigate. The writing committee, consisting of one representative from each organization, is then responsible for going back to the parent organizations and collecting any information related to the specific subject under study. Other members of the NJCLD are urged to transmit their ideas to the writing committee prior to the next annual meeting. One day before that meeting, the writing committee meets for a full day and develops the first draft of what will ultimately become a position paper. (I would be remiss at this point if I did not offer a special accolade to Anthony Bashir, representing ASHA, who has been on the writing committee from the start and who has done a tremendous job in keeping that committee on task at all times.)

The preliminary draft is brought before the entire NJCLD for reaction, discussion, revision, or rejection. The revised draft is then sent back to the parent organizations for their evaluation and continued input. At the next meeting of the writing committee, these suggestions and others are incorporated into still another draft. This document is once more reviewed by the NJCLD, and the process is repeated until the paper is ready for approval.

It is the policy of the NJCLD that formal action to accept position papers can not be taken unless each member organization has had a representative present at the time formal action or voting was taken. Position papers are approved by a three-fourths vote of the NJCLD member organizations, each organization having a single vote. Those papers that are approved are published as official documents of the NJCLD after *at least* one review by the member organizations. Some papers, such as the statement on definition, take over 2 years before final acceptance.

In recent years the NJCLD also has disseminated a document that is different from a position paper. The purpose of this document, referred to as a *statement,* is to provide a collective reaction to current issues in a more timely fashion. A statement is developed in the same way as a paper; however, the approval process differs substantially. For a statement, the representatives of each member organization vote on the document (i.e., each member organization has one vote). It does not go back to each organization for approval from these bodies.

With regard to dissemination, the NJCLD has always been anxious to have its statements given as much visibility as possible. We have hoped that, as textbooks and other books are revised, the position papers and statements could be included or their availability made known. At the same time, it is the policy of the committee that if any member organization of NJCLD, or appointed representatives of those organizations, present for publication position papers or other formal NJCLD statements, the NJCLD shall be acknowledged appropriately in the title and cited as the author.

CONCLUSION

The National Joint Committee on Learning Disabilities has always believed its primary objective to be the effecting of greater unity and cooperation among all the organizations that are primarily involved in the diagnosis, remediation, and treatment of individuals suffering with this serious disorder. In the early stages of its development, the NJCLD was plagued by issues of polarity, territorial imperatives, and plain old-fashioned narcissism. The NJCLD has matured in infinite ways over the many years of its existence. I [Jules Abrams] now perceive the NJCLD as moving into the psychological period of young adulthood. Some of the most difficult issues related to assessment and eligibility for services are now in the process of being studied. There is an increasing emphasis on research-based documents. Official papers and statements are reviewed by the NJCLD every 5 years to determine currentness and need for change. With increasing scientific rigor and mutual respect among its members as professionals, the NJCLD continues to accomplish its mission.

REFERENCE

Education for All Handicapped Children Act of 1975, 20 U.S.C. § 1400 *et seq.*

Documents

THE NJCLD POSITION PAPERS, STATEMENTS, AND REPORTS were developed to provide a timely response to national issues concerning learning disabilities. All approved documents are provided in their entirety and are organized for ease of use according to general categories. Within each topical area, the papers are presented in reverse chronological order so that the most current papers occur first. However, this convention is not followed in the "Basic Issues" section. Since the NJCLD paper on definition is cited frequently, a decision was made to begin this section with the paper on the current definition. The date when a particular position paper, statement, and report was approved is also provided on the title page of each document.

Basic Issues

Learning Disabilities: Issues on Definition

A Position Paper of the
National Joint Committee
on Learning Disabilities
Revised January, 1990

ENACTMENT OF THE EDUCATION FOR ALL HANDICAPPED CHILDREN Act (PL 94-142) mandated changes in the assessment and education of individuals with varying disabilities. The Act provides the basis for securing a systematic methodology for the identification, assessment, and education of children and youth with disabilities. Of specific interest to the National Joint Committee on Learning Disabilities (NJCLD) are those individuals identified categorically within the Law as having learning disabilities.

Federal regulations state that an individual may have a learning disability when a severe discrepancy exists between achievement and intellectual ability in one or more of the following areas: oral expression, listening comprehension, written expression, basic reading skills, reading comprehension, mathematical calculation, and mathematical reasoning. While the law and regulations have specified the areas of deficits that constitute learning disabilities, there remain widespread problems with the definition, methods for identifying the individuals to be served, and problems in delineating the assessment team's membership and responsibilities. The following statement of the NJCLD addresses problems resulting from the Federal definition of learning disabilities.

THE DEFINITION OF LEARNING DISABILITIES

In 1967, the National Advisory Committee on Handicapped Children (NACHC) developed a definition of learning disabilities, a definition that is quoted widely and is included in PL 94-142.

> "Specific learning disability" means a disorder in one or more of the basic psychological processes involved in understanding or in using language, spoken or written, which may manifest itself in an imperfect ability to listen, think, speak, read, write, spell, or to do mathematical calculations. The term includes such conditions as perceptual handicaps, brain injury, minimal brain dysfunction, dyslexia, and developmental aphasia. The term does not include children who have learning problems which are primarily the result of visual, hearing, or motor handicaps, of mental retardation, of emotional disturbance, or of environmental, cultural, or economic disadvantage.

While other definitions of learning disabilities exist among different professional organizations and state education agencies, it was the NACHC definition that provided the basis for legislation and funding that resulted in the establishment of education programs for children with learning disabilities and programs for the preparation of professionals. Numerous positive effects have been realized through the definition and general goals of PL 94-142. However, interpretation of the definition has resulted in a series of problems that have affected theoretical and service-delivery issues in learning disabilities. Some of these issues include the following:

1. The Federal definition of learning disabilities frequently has been misinterpreted. This has led many people to regard those with learning disabilities as a homogeneous group of individuals. This conclusion is clearly erroneous. The definition also has led to the belief that a standard approach to assessment and educational management exists for individuals with learning disabilities. Practices related to identification, assessment, and remediation were keyed to this misinterpretation of the definition with resulting confusion in these areas.

The NJCLD urges that "learning disabilities" be recognized as a general term referring to a heterogeneous group of disorders. These disorders are realized as significant difficulties in the acquisition and use of one or more of the following functions: listening, speaking, reading, writing, reasoning, and mathematical abilities.

Individuals with such disabilities also may evidence problems in their ability to self-regulate behaviors and demonstrate altered patterns of social perception and social interaction. The idea that these problems can exist with learning disabilities has been acknowledged by the NJCLD and is consistent with current research findings. The inclusion of this idea within the definition is, therefore, timely and contributes to a better understanding of individuals with learning disabilities. However, the NJCLD does not believe or support the argument that problems of self-regulation, social perception and/or interaction alone constitute a learning disability.

Furthermore, the fact that the learning disabled population includes different subgroups of individuals can no longer be ignored. An integration of the results of past and current research and clinical-educational experience related to these subgroups is essential to identifying the "who" in learning disabilities.

2. The use of "children" in the federal definition limits the applicability of the term 'learning disabilities' to individuals 0–21 years of age. This results in a failure to recognize the developmental nature of learning disabilities. Indeed, learning disabilities must be viewed as a problem not only of the school years, but of early childhood and continuing into adult life. It is, therefore, a problem that may occur across the life span.

NOTES

3. The etiology of learning disabilities is not stated clearly within the federal definition but is implied by a listing of terms and disorders. The NJCLD urges that the disorders represented by the collective term "learning disabilities" are understood as intrinsic to the individual and that the basis of the disorders is presumed to be due to central nervous system dysfunction. Although the NJCLD supports the idea that failure to learn or to attain curricular expectations occurs for diverse reasons, learning disabilities have their basis in inherently altered processes of acquiring and using information. It is essential to understand this notion if one is to appreciate the resultant interaction between the learner and the learning environments. An understanding of this interaction facilitates the development of effective service delivery models and adaptive curriculum. This also leads to a clearer understanding of the ways in which individuals with learning disabilities may interact in a life-long social and cultural milieu.

The NJCLD believes that the idea of central nervous system dysfunction as a basis for learning disabilities is appropriate. This must not, however, restrict the identification of a learning disability to the physician. In fact, many individuals with manifest central nervous system dysfunction, such as individuals with cerebral palsy, do not necessarily evidence learning disorders. For the individual with learning disabilities, evidence of central nervous system dysfunction may or may not be elicited during the course of a medical-neurological examination. The critical elements in the diagnosis of learning disabilities are elicited during psychological, educational and/or language assessments.

An understanding of etiological mechanisms (a) facilitates a determination of prognosis, (b) provides information to individuals and their families that helps to clarify their understanding of the manifest disorder(s), and (c) provides direction to research studies that will influence educational practice.

4. The wording of the "exclusion clause" in the Federal definition of learning disabilities lends itself to the misinterpretation that individuals with learning disabilities cannot be multihandicapped or be from different cultural and linguistic backgrounds. It is essential to understand and recognize the learning disabilities as they might occur within the varying disability categories as well as different cultural and linguistic groups. Individuals within these groups frequently have received inappropriate educational assessment, planning, and instruction because they could not be identified as learning disabled.

The NJCLD supports the idea that learning disabilities are not the primary and direct result of other disabilities and should not be so confused. However, the NJCLD notes specifically that learning disabilities may occur concomitantly with other disabilities. Although these individuals may be served educationally through different service modes, a denial of the existence of significant learning disabilities will result in inappropriate assessment and educational instruction and can result in the denial of direct or indirect professional services.

5. In addition to changes made in the 1981 definition related to social behavior, the following changes were made to clarify or simplify the language of the definition.

1. The word "generic" was changed to "general."

2. The term "environmental influences" was changed to "extrinsic influences."

3. The phrase "social and emotional disturbance" was changed to "serious emotional disturbance."

4. The word "direct" was deleted.

In the light of the preceding discussion, the NJCLD recommends the following definition of learning disabilities:

Learning disabilities is a general term that refers to a heterogeneous group of disorders manifested by significant difficulties in the acquisition and use of listening, speaking, reading, writing, reasoning, or mathematical abilities. These disorders are intrinsic to the individual, presumed to be due to central nervous system dysfunction, and may occur across the life span. Problems in self-regulatory behaviors, social perception, and social interaction may exist with learning disabilities but do not by themselves constitute a learning disability. Although learning disabilities may occur concomitantly with other handicapping conditions (for example, sensory impairment, mental retardation, serious emotional disturbance), or with extrinsic influences (such as cultural differences, insufficient or inappropriate instruction), they are not the result of those conditions or influences.

Note. In January 1981, the NJCLD developed a new definition of learning disabilities that was adopted by all member organizations except the Learning Disabilities Association of America. The 1981 definition reads as follows:

Learning disabilities is a generic term that refers to a heterogeneous group of disorders manifested by significant difficulties in the acquisition and use of listening, speaking, reading, writing, reasoning, or mathematical abilities. These disorders are intrinsic to the individual and presumed to be due to central nervous system dysfunction. Even though a learning disability may occur concomitantly with other handicapping conditions (e.g., sensory impairment, mental retardation, social and emotional disturbance), or environmental influences (e.g., cultural differences, insufficient/inappropriate instruction, psychogenic factors), it is not the direct result of those conditions or influences.

In the following years, the NJCLD continued to review the literature and practice related to defining and identifying individuals with learning disabilities. As a result of new information available in the literature, the NJCLD revised its 1981 definition. The revised definition has been formally adopted as the official definition of learning disabilities by the following NJCLD member organizations: American Speech-Language-Hearing Association, Council for Learning Disabilities, Division for Children with Communication Disorders, International Reading Association, Learning Disabilities Association, National Association of School Psychologists, and Orton Dyslexia Society. The Division for Learning Disabilities has taken no action on the definition.

REFERENCE

Education for All Handicapped Children Act of 1975, 20 U.S.C. § 1400 *et seq.*

Learning Disabilities: Issues on Definition[1]

**A Position Paper of the National Joint Committee on Learning Disabilities
January, 1981**

---

[1]This paper was revised in 1990 and is provided on page 27. All current reference to the NJCLD's position on definition should be made to the 1990 position paper.

THE ENACTMENT OF PL 94-142 HAS RIGHTLY MANDATED CHANGES in the assessment and education of individuals with varying handicapping conditions. The law has provided the basis for securing a systematic methodology for the identification, assessment, and education of children with handicaps. Of specific interest to the National Joint Committee on Learning Disabilities (NJCLD) are those individuals identified categorically within the law as having learning disabilities.

Federal regulations state that an individual may have a learning disability when a severe discrepancy exists between achievement and intellectual ability in one or more of the following areas: oral expression, listening comprehension, written expression, basic reading skills, reading comprehension, mathematical calculation, and mathematical reasoning. While the law and regulations have specified the areas of deficits that constitute learning disabilities, there remain widespread problems with the definition, methods for identifying the individuals to be served, and problems in delineating the assessment team's membership and responsibilities. The following position paper of the NJCLD addresses problems resulting from the Federal definition of learning disabilities.

THE DEFINITION OF LEARNING DISABILITIES

In 1967 the National Advisory Committee on Handicapped Children (NACHC) developed a definition of learning disabilities, a definition that is quoted widely and is included in PL 94-142.

> "Specific learning disability" means a disorder in one or more of the basic psychological processes involved in understanding or in using language, spoken or written, which may manifest itself in an imperfect ability to listen, think, speak, read, write, spell, or to do mathematical calculations. The term includes such conditions as perceptual handicaps, brain injury, minimal brain dysfunction, dyslexia, and developmental aphasia. The term does not include children who have learning problems which are primarily the result of visual, hearing, or motor handicaps, of mental retardation, of emotional disturbance, or of environmental, cultural, or economic disadvantage.

While other definitions of learning disabilities exist among different professional organizations and state education agencies, it was the NACHC definition that provided the basis for legislation and funding that resulted in the establishment of education programs for children with learning disabilities and programs for the training of professionals. Numerous positive effects have been realized through the definition and general goals of PL 94-142. However, interpretation of the definition has resulted in a series of problems that have affected theoretical and service-delivery issues in learning disabilities. Some of these issues include the following:

1. The federal definition of learning disabilities frequently has been misinterpreted. This has led many people to regard those with learning disabilities as a homogeneous group of individuals. This conclusion is clearly erroneous. The definition also has led to the belief that a standard approach to assessment and educational management exists for individuals with learning disabilities. Practices related to identification, assessment, and remediation were keyed to this misinterpretation of the definition with resulting confusion in these areas.

The NJCLD urges that "learning disabilities" be recognized as a general term referring to a heterogeneous group of disorders. These disorders are realized as significant difficulties in the acquisition and use of one or more of the following functions: listening, speaking, reading, writing, reasoning, and mathematical abilities. Individuals with such disabilities may also evidence problems in their ability to self-regulate behaviors and demonstrate altered patterns of social perception and social interaction. Furthermore, the fact that the learning disabled population includes different subgroups of individuals can no longer be ignored. An integration of the results of past and current research and clinical-educational experience related to these subgroups is essential to identifying the "who" in learning disabilities.

2. The use of "children" in the federal definition limits the applicability of the term "learning disabilities" to individuals 0–21 years of age. This results in a failure to recognize the developmental nature of learning disabilities. Indeed, learning disabilities must be viewed as a problem not only of the school years, but of early childhood and continuing into adult life.

3. The etiology of learning disabilities is not stated clearly within the federal definition but is implied by a listing of terms and disorders. The NJCLD urges that the disorders represented by the collective term "learning disabilities" are understood as intrinsic to the individual and that the basis of the disorders is presumed to be due to central nervous system dysfunction. Although the NJCLD supports the idea that failure to learn or to attain curricular expectations occurs for diverse reasons, learning disabilities have their basis

in inherently altered processes of acquiring and using information. It is essential to understand this notion if one is to appreciate the resultant interaction between the learner and the learning environments. An understanding of this interaction facilitates the development of effective service delivery models and adaptive curriculum. This also leads to a clearer understanding of the ways in which individuals with learning disabilities may interact in a life-long social and cultural milieu.

The NJCLD believes that the idea of central nervous system dysfunction as a basis for learning disabilities is appropriate. This must not, however, restrict the identification of a learning disability to the physician. In fact, many individuals with manifest central nervous system dysfunction, such as individuals with cerebral palsy, do not necessarily evidence learning disorders. For the individual with learning disabilities, evidence of central nervous system dysfunction may or may not be elicited during the course of a medical-neurological examination. The critical elements in the diagnosis of learning disabilities are elicited during psychological, educational and/or language assessments.

An understanding of etiological mechanisms (a) facilitates a determination of prognosis, (b) provides information to individuals and their families that helps to clarify their understanding of the manifest disorder(s), and (c) provides direction for research studies that will influence educational practice.

4. The wording of the "exclusion clause" in the Federal definition of learning disabilities lends itself to the misinterpretation that individuals with learning disabilities cannot be multihandicapped or be from different cultural and linguistic backgrounds. It is essential to understand and recognize the learning disabilities as they might occur within varying handicapping conditions as well as different cultural and linguistic groups. Individuals within these groups frequently have received inappropriate educational assessment, planning, and instruction because they could not be identified as learning disabled.

The NJCLD supports the idea that learning disabilities are not the primary and direct result of other handicapping conditions and should not be so confused. However, the NJCLD notes specifically that learning disabilities may occur concomitantly with other handicapping conditions. Although these individuals may be served educationally through different service modes, a denial of the existence of significant learning disabilities will result in inappropriate assessment and educational instruction and can result in the denial of direct or indirect professional services.

In light of the preceding discussion the NJCLD recommends the following definition of learning disabilities:

Learning disabilities is a generic term that refers to a heterogeneous group of disorders manifested by significant difficulties in the acquisition and use of listening, speaking, reading, writing, reasoning, or mathematical abilities. These disorders are intrinsic to the individual and presumed to be due to central nervous dysfunction. Even though a learning disability may occur concomitantly with other handicapping conditions (e.g., sensory impairment, mental retardation, social and emotional disturbance) or environmental influences (e.g., cultural differences, insufficient/inappropriate instruction, psychogenic factors), it is not the direct result of those conditions or influences.

REFERENCE

Education for All Handicapped Children Act of 1975, 20 U.S.C. § 1400 *et seq*.

This paper was revised in 1990 and is provided on page 27. All current reference to the NJCLD's position on definition should be made to the 1990 position paper.

Operationalizing the NJCLD Definition of Learning Disabilities for Ongoing Assessment in Schools

A Position Paper of the
National Joint Committee
on Learning Disabilities
February 1, 1997

IN MEMORY OF SAMUEL A. KIRK, ONE OF THE FATHERS OF special education to whom we all owe so much.

NJCLD DEFINITION AND ITS FIVE CONSTRUCTS

The purposes of this paper are to highlight five constructs underlying the National Joint Committee on Learning Disabilities (NJCLD) definition of learning disabilities and to recommend operational procedures for ongoing assessment and interventions for children in preschool through secondary school. This paper builds on previous statements and papers of the NJCLD. It is organized in two sections: The first presents the definition and the five constructs underlying it; the second describes operational procedures organized according to the five constructs basic to the definition.

THE NJCLD DEFINITION

Learning disabilities is a general term that refers to a heterogeneous group of disorders manifested by significant difficulties in the acquisition and use of listening, speaking, reading, writing, reasoning, or mathematical skills.

These disorders are intrinsic to the individual, presumed to be due to central nervous system dysfunction, and may occur across the life span. Problems in self-regulatory behaviors, social perception, and social interaction may exist with learning disabilities but do not, by themselves, constitute a learning disability.

Although learning disabilities may occur concomitantly with other disabilities (e.g., sensory impairment, mental retardation, serious emotional disturbance), or with extrinsic influences (such as cultural differences, insufficient or inappropriate instruction), they are not the result of those conditions or influences (see the paper "Learning Disabilities: Issues on Definition," 1990, in this book).

THE FIVE CONSTRUCTS

1. Learning disabilities are heterogeneous, both within and across individuals. Intraindividual differences involve varied profiles of learning strength and need and/or shifts across the life span within individuals. Interindividual differences involve different manifestations of learning disabilities for different individuals.

2. Learning disabilities result in significant difficulties in the acquisition and use of listening, speaking, reading, writing, reasoning, and/or mathematical skills. Such difficulties are evident when an individual's appropriate levels of effort do not result in reasonable progress given the opportunity for effective educational instruction and with the recognition that all individuals learn at a different pace and with differing effort. Significant difficulty cannot be determined solely by a quantitative test score.

3. Learning disabilities are intrinsic to the individual. They are presumed to be related to differences in central nervous system development. They do not disappear over time, but may range in expression and severity at different life stages.

4. Learning disabilities may occur concomitantly with other disabilities that do not, by themselves, constitute a learning disability. For example, difficulty with self-regulatory behaviors, social perception, and social interactions may occur for many reasons. Some social interaction problems result from learning disabilities; others do not. Individuals with other disabilities, such as sensory impairments, attention deficit hyperactivity disorders, mental retardation, and serious emotional disturbance, may also have learning disabilities, but such conditions do not cause or constitute learning disabilities.

5. Learning disabilities are not caused by extrinsic influences. Inconsistent or insufficient instruction or a lack of instructional experience cause learning difficulties, but not learning disabilities. However, individuals who have had inconsistent or insufficient instruction may also have learning disabilities. The challenge is to document that inadequate or insufficient instruction is not the primary cause of a learning disability. Individuals from all cultural and linguistic backgrounds may also have learning disabilities; therefore, assessments must be designed acknowledging this diversity in culture and language, and examiners who test children from each background must be sensitive to such factors and use practices that are individualized and appropriate for each child.

FOUR STEPS OF ONGOING ASSESSMENT

The NJCLD recommends a four-step procedure for operationalizing the definition to determine the presence of learning disabilities and to make decisions for eligibility for and provision of special education and related services.

Step 1. Describe learning problems prior to referral for formal assessment.

Purpose. The purposes of Step 1 are to define problems raised by parents, teachers, or students themselves [Note: In this document, "parents" means parents, guardians, or others assuming a parental role.]; to consider the history of those concerns; to identify, evaluate, (see the paper "Learning Disabilities and the Preschool Child," 1985, in this book) and modify extrinsic factors that may be contributing to the problems; and to begin interventions and accommodations with consultation from a problem-solving team that includes the student's classroom teacher, other teachers and specialists, the parent, and the student when appropriate. The members of the problem-solving team come together based on their collective knowledge of, and experience with, the student involved, and with the relevant instructional contexts.

Key Questions

1. What are the student's learning strengths and problems?

2. How do the strengths and problems vary within the educational environment, both academic and nonacademic?

3. What interventions and accommodations, as well as modifications of typical teaching strategies, might help the student learn?

Process. When a student is having a problem that involves significant difficulty in the acquisition and use of listening, speaking, writing, reasoning, or mathematical abilities, a problem-solving process should begin. The process should enable the student, teachers, other professionals, and the parent to define the learning problem and variations within multiple contexts. This should be a collaborative, student-centered process that results in the implementation of interventions and accommodations designed to meet the student's needs. The options should exist along a continuum of support for the student, teacher, and parent, ranging from minimal consultation and accommodations to extensive interventions. The responsibilities of the team are to:

1. Interview key participants about their perceptions of the problem (at least the student, parents, and teachers).

2. Gather and analyze information about the classroom and the student's performance in the areas of concern identified by the participants, for example, by:

(a) Observing and describing the classroom and the student's performance using naturalistic and curriculum-based samples;

(b) Reviewing school records and developmental and educational history;

(c) Reviewing individual portfolios.

3. Consider alternative explanations for the student's learning problems or learning differences, including:

(a) Insufficient or inappropriate instruction;

(b) Related factors that are important to consider, but do not by themselves constitute learning disabilities, including:
- Self-regulatory behaviors (e.g., attention, motivation, and impulsivity do not by themselves constitute learning disabilities, but self-regulation of behaviors for performing language, academic, or educational tasks may be an integral part of a learning disability);
- Social perception (e.g., inappropriate social judgments are not learning disabilities, but they may be the secondary consequences of the learning disabilities);
- Social interaction (e.g., problems relating to peers do not by themselves constitute learning disability, but in some cases may be secondary to learning disabilities);

(c) Other disabilities such as:
- Sensory impairments (requiring screening for hearing or visual deficits);
- Mental retardation or general cognitive disabilities;
- Serious emotional disturbance.

(d) Cultural and linguistic differences must not be misconstrued as learning problems or learning disabilities.

4. Brainstorm solutions (e.g., interventions, accommodations, diagnostic teaching, environmental modifications, immediate referral for evaluation).

5. Recommend and implement interventions and/or accommodations to meet the student's needs (e.g., if the team identifies a problem in phonemic awareness that might put the student at risk for future reading problems, intervention should be provided promptly instead of waiting for the student to fail).

6. Monitor the interventions and accommodations and make adjustments as needed.

7. Evaluate the effectiveness of interventions and accommodations.

Decision-Making Alternatives

1. If the problem-solving process is effective, provide ongoing educational interventions and accommodations and continue to modify them as necessary; do not, however, refer at this time for formal evaluation.

2. If the problem-solving process is not effective, consider whether appropriate or sufficient interventions and accommodations have been tried or, even if they have not, whether a disability is suspected that may require special education and related services; if so, proceed to referral for formal evaluation for special education and related services.

Summary. Step 1 is a problem-solving and supportive process that provides an opportunity for analyzing the student's problems, for conducting informal contextually focused assessment, for probing what works and what does not, and for providing individualized interventions aimed at addressing the needs of the student. The purpose is to solve problems expediently, but if they cannot be solved with general resources, to move into the next step in a timely fashion, using the findings from Step 1 as an informational base.

Step 2. Identify individuals as having learning disabilities.

Purpose. This step incorporates the information from Step 1 with results from additional informal and formal assessments to describe the characteristics of the learner and the pervasiveness and severity of the problems in order to diagnose learning disabilities through a comprehensive evaluation.

Key Questions

1. What is the nature of the learning problems and how pervasive and severe are they?

2. Is performance in the problem areas unexpectedly low compared with the student's performance in other areas?

3. Are the learning problems the result of learning disabilities (as opposed to some other explanation)?

Process. The evaluation is conducted by a multidisciplinary team of qualified professionals who collaborate to make a diagnosis based on consideration of strengths as well as weaknesses in the pertinent areas of listening, speaking, reading, writing, reasoning, or mathematical abilities. The unexpectedly low performance should be in relation to the student's age, instructional history, cognitive abilities, and performance in other academic areas, based on multiple measures. Step 2 requires the following recommended activities:

1. Identify specific aspects of listening, speaking, reading, writing, reasoning, or mathematical abilities that are interfering with learning progress given the student's educational opportunities.

   (a) This comprehensive evaluation should include a variety of assessments and procedures such as:
   - Review of data from case history, interviews, and direct observations;
   - Standardized tests that are reliable, valid, and have current and age-appropriate normative data;
   - Contextual-based assessment;
   - Task and error pattern analysis;
   - Diagnostic teaching;
   - Other nonstandardized approaches.

   (b) The comprehensive evaluation should include recognition that learning disabilities, like other disabilities, vary in their manifestations, such that:
   - Learning disabilities involve varied patterns of strength and difficulty across and within the pertinent areas;
   - Learning disabilities range in expression and severity, varying with the demands of life stage and different contexts, but all have significant life effects;
   - Learning disabilities can appear differently in varied settings, including both academic and nonacademic settings.

   (c) No single test, battery of tests, or list of symptoms is sufficient for the diagnosis of learning disabilities. Appropriate diagnosis depends on the skills, training, and qualifications of the examiners who use the tools and techniques in the evaluation process. The following are examples of patterns that are symptomatic of learning disabilities when they persist even with adequate learning opportunities and in contrast to areas of relative strength:
   - Listening:
     During early development, listening problems might appear as inattention to verbal messages, difficulty understanding familiar words, and sentence and discourse comprehension and retention difficulties;

During the later years, listening problems might appear as difficulty detecting, manipulating, and repeating (orally or in writing) whole words or parts of words, including phonemes; difficulty comprehending the language of others, particularly when complex syntax, abstract meanings, and focused attention are required, or when following directions or taking notes.

- Speaking:

During early development, speaking problems might appear as difficulty learning the linguistic rules for producing words, word endings, grammatical function words, and syntactic structures;

During later years, these problems may persist as difficulties of language formulation and organization; verbal fluency; word retrieval; selection of specific and appropriate vocabulary; judging the needs of listeners for information; judging the style of discourse that is appropriate for particular speaking partners and situations; being appropriately assertive and responsive in varied conversations; sequencing sounds and syllables, particularly in words with multiple syllables and consonant clusters; and associating speech productions with sounds and symbols.

- Reading:

During the emergent literacy periods, reading problems might appear as limited interest in, understanding of, or retelling of written texts;

During the early elementary years, reading problems might appear as difficulty acquiring decoding strategies, including meaning-based prediction, and using these strategies flexibly in interaction with comprehension;

During later elementary and secondary years, reading problems might appear as continued difficulty reading text aloud or silently; difficulty reading text fluently; or with limited understanding, particularly expository texts in content subjects, understanding written directions, or use of figurative language or the language of another time or dialect.

- Writing:

During the emergent literacy period, writing problems might appear as limited interest in and ability to manipulate the tools of writing and to form scribble or letter shapes that imitate adult forms;

During the early elementary years, writing problems might appear as difficulty learning to form and retrieve letters for representing sounds and words and difficulty learning to formulate words, phrases, and sentences in writing;

During later elementary and secondary years, writing problems might appear as limited vocabulary, persistent difficulty with conventions of writing (such as spelling and punctuation); with planning and organizing written texts for a particular audience and purpose; with strategies for organizing an approach to the writing process; and with strategies for reviewing and revising written products.

- Reasoning:
  Across the age span, reasoning problems might appear as problems of executive functioning, verbal and nonverbal reasoning, and cognitive strategies; they include difficulty detecting and/or understanding relationships between objects or their symbolic representations, holding them, translating to other representations, detecting and reporting one or more interpretations, evaluating the interpretive choices to see if they make sense and are consistent with the data, and acting appropriately.

- Mathematical ability:
  During early development, mathematical ability problems might appear as difficulty developing numerical concepts, learning rote counting, and acquiring concepts underlying numerical or verbal symbols that relate to quantitative reasoning;

  During elementary and secondary school, difficulties might involve skills for retaining and reproducing an orderly sequence of mathematical operations; understanding mathematical concepts and relationships; retaining, recalling, and applying computational facts and procedures; grasping quantitative relationships explained in words; analyzing mathematical problems, devising and implementing an orderly approach to solving them, making estimates, performing computations, checking the results, and evaluating whether they make sense in the context of the problem;

  During later stages, difficulties might be evident primarily as problems of abstract quantitative thinking.

2. Investigate processing differences in the specific area of concern. Indicators include cognitive and integrative problems, such as those described above, as well as difficulties involving perception, memory, focused attention, temporal sequencing, motor planning and coordination, flexibility in thinking, reasoning, and organization.

3. Consider all evidence, including qualitative data and intra-individual differences within the learner's strengths and weaknesses. Cognitive ability/achievement discrepancies should be used cautiously because learning disability can exist when a numerical discrepancy does not. Such comparisons may assist in the diagnostic process. Careful diagnosticians examine all information and recognize developmental factors, including age and academic experience, in making a determination as to the value of such discrepancies.

4. Avoid overidentification by considering other specific factors that may contribute to the nature and severity of learning disabilities, but do not by themselves constitute learning disabilities (see points under Step 1). Careful formulation and interpretation of diagnostic material is necessary to distinguish learning disabilities from other factors that are manifested by difficulties in learning. Extrinsic blocks to learning, such as inadequate instruction, should also be addressed. Adverse physical, emotional, social, and environmental conditions require a complex of school and community interventions to prevent underachievement. Ignoring such blocks to learning may result in unnecessary referrals for special education and related services.

5. Avoid overidentification by using procedures that are sensitive to the effects of sociocultural and language differences.

6. Avoid underidentification by considering whether learning disabilities are present in co-occurrence with other disabilities or extrinsic factors. That is, assessment should identify specific factors (such as intermittent or unilateral hearing loss or social-perception difficulties) that, although they are not directly responsible for a learning disability, may occur concomitantly.

  (a) Individuals with other disabilities may have concomitant learning disabilities;

  (b) Linguistic and cultural differences do not preclude the possibility of learning disabilities;

  (c) Inadequate instruction does not preclude the possibility of learning disabilities.

Decision-Making Alternatives

1. If the evidence supports a diagnosis of learning disabilities, move to Step 3, where all assessment information will be considered in making an eligibility decision.

2. If the evidence does not support a diagnosis of learning disabilities, additional considerations might be:

(a) Disability other than learning disabilities might best explain the student's learning problems. If so, appropriate diagnostic and intervention techniques should follow.

(b) Disability may be identified and/or extrinsic factors may provide a better explanation of the learning problem; if so, additional consultation with the student and classroom teacher about appropriate educational strategies and accommodations should follow.

Summary. This is the diagnostic step for identifying a student as having learning disabilities. Learning disabilities are lifelong; therefore, this part of the process need occur only once in a person's life span, although, in some cases, diagnostic study may be repeated. In contrast, determining the need for special education and related services or accommodations (Step 3) may occur at multiple points across the life span.

Step 3. Determine eligibility for special education and related services.

Purpose. This step involves a collaborative process to determine the need for special education and related services. A student might have learning disabilities and yet still not need special education or related services at all points during the school-age years.

Key Question

Given the student's learning disabilities and current performance in important academic and social contexts, does the student require special education and related services at this time?

Process. The initial discussion to determine eligibility should be based on assessment activities to:

1. Document the nature of the problem in learning contexts and in naturalistic social interactions involving listening, speaking,

reading, writing, reasoning, or mathematical abilities (may be based on information gathered in Step 1).

2. Interpret information from assessment activities in Step 2.

3. Judge mismatches between the student's abilities and important learning demands at a particular point in time.

4. Given the student's pattern of strengths and needs, recommend areas to be addressed in intervention planning.

Decision-Making Alternatives

1. Decide that the student is eligible to receive special education and related services and proceed to Step 4.

2. Decide that the student does not currently need special education and related services, but could benefit from consultation services aimed at assisting the student within the general education classroom and curriculum, using information from Steps 1, 2, and 3.

3. Decide that the student does not currently need special education and related services under the Individuals with Disabilities Education Act of 1990 (IDEA), but does require an individual plan under Section 504 of the Rehabilitation Act of 1973.

4. Decide that the student needs no special considerations at the present time.

Summary. Step 3 is to determine the need and eligibility for special education and related services. Determination of need should be followed by Step 4, in which an individualized plan is constructed to meet that need.

Step 4. Bridge assessment to specialized instruction and accommodations.

Purpose. Information gathered in all of the previous steps should be used in the collaborative process to design and implement an individualized education plan (IEP) or other individualized plan. Students with learning disabilities, their parents, and general education teachers are active partners in the collaborative decision-making team, along with special educators and professionals in related services who are knowledgeable about the student, the student's learning disabilities, and generalized and specialized curricular needs.

Key Questions

1. What special education and related services and accommodations should be provided?

2. Based on the entire assessment process, what goals should be targeted on the student's IEP?

3. Is this a time to prepare for special transition (such as preschool to elementary school, elementary school to middle school, middle school to high school, high school to postsecondary education or employment)?

Process. The plan should be based on information about the student's learning strengths, as well as learning disabilities, and on information about mismatches between the student's abilities and the expectations of the educational context. It should be relevant to meeting specific contextually based needs identified in Step 1, 2, and 3. Once an IEP or other individualized program has been written, it should be flexible enough to respond to changes in the student's curriculum-based needs, but specific enough to have measurable outcomes. Such a process should involve equal and collaborative participation of members of the team, especially students with learning disabilities and their parents. Activities of the process include the following:

1. Describe the student's current strengths, weaknesses, and learning styles, using input from all participants, including the parent and student.

2. Analyze information obtained in Steps 1 through 3 to ensure that all areas of concern are addressed and to serve as the starting point to measure progress and to evaluate the effectiveness of the IEP. This discussion should focus on how the student's learning disability affects the student within the educational environment including academic, vocational, and nonacademic areas. This may include discussions of the student's learning style and a description of those techniques and/or materials that have proven effective or ineffective.

3. Establish final outcomes of the student's program. Take time to articulate those behaviors and skills that one would expect from the student on exiting special education or school. This will assist the team in addressing transitional services the student may need and setting long-term goals for the student.

4. Establish annual goals in the student's IEP based on knowledge of where the student is now and hopes to be in the future. A goal

should be written for each area of concern and the goals should be prioritized. Remember that, besides academic skills, goals can address skills that will help the student be independent in school/work habits, learning strategies, or organizational skills.

5. Establish objectives to assist the team to reach each identified goal. These are the intermediate steps between where the student is now and the annual goal. Each objective should have an evaluation procedure, criteria, and schedule for meeting the objective.

6. Use information from ongoing evaluation procedures to help the team evaluate the effectiveness of the IEP. These procedures can include portfolios, observations, student projects, and oral presentations. This information can be used in an IEP meeting, at least annually, to revise or rewrite a student's IEP.

Conduct reevaluation activities at 3-year intervals (or less) and at meaningful transition points that include preschool to elementary, elementary to middle school, middle school to high school and beyond high school. The reevaluation should focus on the student's progress and the ongoing need for special education and related services rather than on redundant identification of the individual as having learning disabilities, considering the following: (a) the effectiveness of special education and related services, accommodations, and environmental modifications; (b) the continuing need for those services; and (c) recommendations related to periods of transition. At any point when a decision is made to discontinue special education and related services, a plan should be developed to keep necessary modifications, accommodations, and interventions in place. The determination of the continued need for special education and related services, accommodations, and environmental modifications (Step 3) should be based on several factors, including both formal and informal assessments.

Decision-Making Alternatives

1. Review and revise the educational program as needed, which may include minor or major program changes based on the evaluation of the student's progress and the effectiveness of the interventions used.

2. Determine that special education and related services are not currently needed, but plan for periodic review of the student's educational progress.

Summary. Step 4 involves developing a plan, implementing it, and judging the effectiveness of special education and related services so that modifications can be made as needed.

SUMMARY

Ongoing assessment throughout the school years is critical to develop the educational potential of all children, especially those with learning disabilities. School personnel, parents, and students should proceed with as much information as possible, giving consideration to individual skills and academic needs. The five constructs of the NJCLD definition of learning disabilities can serve as a guide to this process.

REFERENCES

Individuals with Disabilities Education Act of 1990, 20 U.S.C. § 1400 *et seq.*

Rehabilitation Act of 1973, 29 U.S.C. § 701 *et seq.*

Note. The following National Joint Committee on Learning Disabilities papers were cited in or consulted for this paper, and can be found in this book:

"Issues in the Delivery of Services to Individuals with Learning Disabilities," 1982

"Learning Disabilities and the Preschool Child," 1985

"Issues in Learning Disabilities: Assessment and Diagnosis," 1987

"Learning Disabilities: Issues on Definition," 1990

Issues in Learning Disabilities: Assessment and Diagnosis

A Position Paper of the
National Joint Committee
on Learning Disabilities
September, 1987

THE NATIONAL JOINT COMMITTEE ON LEARNING DISABILITIES (NJCLD) believes that inappropriate diagnostic practices and procedures have contributed to misclassification of individuals and questionable incidence rates of learning disabilities. Such practices and procedures result in erroneously including individuals whose learning and behavioral problems are not attributable to learning disabilities and excluding individuals whose deficits are manifestations of specific learning disabilities.

The NJCLD views the following issues as important to an understanding of current concerns:

- lack of adherence to a consistent definition of learning disabilities that emphasizes the intrinsic and life-long nature of the condition;

- lack of understanding, acceptance, and willingness to accommodate normal variations in learning and behavior;

- lack of sufficient competent personnel and appropriate programs to support the efforts of teachers to accommodate the needs of children who do not have learning disabilities but who require alternative instructional methods;

- insufficient supply of competently prepared professionals to diagnose and manage exceptional individuals;

- the false belief that underachievement is synonymous with specific learning disability;

- the incorrect assumption that quantitative formulas alone can be used to diagnose learning disabilities;

- failure of multidisciplinary teams to consider and integrate findings related to the presenting problem(s);

- lack of comprehensive assessment practices, procedures, and instruments necessary to differentiate learning disabilities from other types of learning problems; and

- general preference for the label "learning disability" over "mental retardation" or "emotional disturbance," which leads to the misclassification of some individuals.

The NJCLD addresses these concerns in this statement and emphasizes the importance of integrating assessment, diagnosis, and procedures that lead to a diagnosis of learning disability and eligibility for services. Policymakers, educational administrators, regular and special educators, related services personnel, parents, advocates, and others who identify, assess, diagnose, and provide services to people with learning disabilities should find it relevant.

1. Learning Disabilities Are Manifested Differently Over Time, in Severity and in Various Settings.

    a. Learning disabilities, like other handicapping conditions, vary in their manifestations and are mild, moderate, or severe.

    b. Appropriate procedures must be used from early childhood through adulthood to assess and identify individuals suspected of having learning disabilities. Procedures vary with different age groups.

    c. Problems associated with learning disabilities may be observed in both academic and non-academic settings. Consequently, procedures used to diagnose individuals should include data collected from all relevant settings.

    d. Individuals who manifest specific symptoms of—or who are considered at risk for—learning disabilities should be monitored by qualified personnel to determine if assessment or other special services are needed. This is especially true for children under the age of nine.

2. Differential Diagnosis Is Necessary to Distinguish Between and Among Other Disorders, Syndromes, and Factors That Can Interfere with the Acquisition and Use of Listening, Speaking, Reading, Writing, Reasoning, or Mathematical Abilities.

    a. Differential diagnosis is a process and requires the formulation of hypotheses regarding the etiology and nature of the presenting problem. When one of several factors may be the cause of learning problems, low achievement, underachievement, or maladaptive behavior, all possible etiological alternatives must be considered.

    b. Intellectual limitations, sensory impairments, and adverse emotional, social and environmental conditions may be the primary cause of *low achievement* and should not be confused with learning disabilities.

    c. Documentation of *underachievement* in one or more areas is a necessary but insufficient criterion for the diagnosis of learning disabilities.

    d. Diagnosis of learning disabilities must be based on an analysis of the individual's strengths as well as weaknesses.

    e. Linguistic and cultural differences, inadequate instruction, and/or social-emotional deprivation do not preclude the possibility that an individual also has a learning disability. Similarly, individuals with other handicapping conditions, such as mental retardation, sensory impairments, autism, or severe emotional or behavioral disturbances may have concomitant learning disabilities.

    f. Diagnostic judgments must not depend solely on test results. Such a practice can cause over-reliance on test scores, inadequate consideration of individual behavioral and social characteristics, and insufficient integration of other assessment information.

    g. Discrepancy formulas must not be used as the only criterion for the diagnosis of learning disabilities.

    h. Scores on intelligence tests (IQs) are not the only reflection of intellectual ability. Diagnostic criteria based exclusively on IQ disregard intra-individual differences in skills and performance.

    i. Manifestations of learning disabilities, such as language impairment, can reduce performance on intelligence tests. Therefore, selection of tests and interpretation of results must acknowledge the influence of specific disabilities on intelligence measures.

3. A Comprehensive Assessment Is Needed for Diagnosis and for Planning an Appropriate Intervention Program.

    a. Assessment includes a variety of activities and procedures intended to ensure a comprehensive set of data for determining an individual's status and needs.

b. The procedures used to assess learning disabilities should address the presenting problems.

c. A comprehensive assessment must include procedures to determine levels of performance in the following domains: motor, sensory, cognitive, communication, and behavior. When a learning disability is suspected, the following areas should be assessed: listening, speaking, reading, writing, reasoning, mathematics, and social skills. However, the assessment must focus on the presenting problem(s) and possible correlate(s).

d. Data from case history, interviews, and direct observations are important sources of information especially when provided by parents, educators, and the individual with the suspected learning disability. The information helps to evaluate signs, symptoms, and behaviors in a historical perspective.

e. Standardized tests must be reliable, valid, and have current normative data. Strict adherence to procedures for administering, scoring, and interpreting tests must be maintained. Performance should be expressed in scores that have the highest degree of comparability across measures, i.e., standard scores should be used rather than grade or age equivalents. Formulas must include a correction for regression if used to calculate a discrepancy between aptitude and achievement.

f. Curriculum based assessment, task and error pattern analysis, diagnostic teaching, and other nonstandardized approaches are viable sources of additional information, especially when data are not available through standardized testing.

g. Information and data collected during the assessment must be used to formulate the intervention plan. That plan must address the entire range and all degrees of severity of the problem identified.

h. Intervention and services should be based on a determination of the individual's present level of performance and functional needs. Program planning should include appropriate provisions for social, personal, vocational, and independent living needs.

4. A Multidisciplinary Team Is Necessary for Assessing, Diagnosing, and Determining Provision of Services.

   a. A multidisciplinary team is essential for making a diagnosis of learning disabilities. Members of the team must possess the range of competencies necessary to assess and make diagnostic decisions.

   b. Assessment data for determining the individual's status and needs are derived from multiple sources. The multidisciplinary team reviews, integrates, and interprets results from these sources, and formulates service options as well.

   c. Individuals who have conducted the assessments must be present when the diagnostic decisions are made. As plans for specific programs and services are developed, parents and those professionals involved in providing direct services should be included on the team. The individual with a learning disability also should be included when appropriate.

5. A Clear Distinction Must Be Made Between "Diagnosis of Learning Disability" and "Eligibility for Specific Services."

   a. Diagnosis of learning disabilities should never be denied to an individual because the specific eligibility criteria for a given program have not been met.

   b. When a diagnosis of learning disabilities is made, appropriate services must be provided.

   c. Programs for individuals with learning disabilities should not be used as placement alternatives for those with other learning and behavioral problems.

   d. The availability of funding must not influence the determination of eligibility for services.

   e. It is improper to deliberately diagnose an individual as learning disabled to generate funds.

The NJCLD recommends that all agencies and individuals concerned with the assessment and diagnosis of learning disabilities carefully consider the issues presented in this paper. The committee believes strongly that adherence to the principles and practices included in this statement will result in appropriate assessment and diagnosis of individuals with learning disabilities.

REFERENCE

National Joint Committee on Learning Disabilities. (1982). Learning disabilities: Issues on definition. *Asha, 24*(11), 945–947.

National Joint Committee on Learning Disabilities. (1983). Inservice programs in learning disabilities. *Asha, 25*(11), 47–49.

National Joint Committee on Learning Disabilities. (1985a). Adults with learning disabilities: A call for action. *Asha, 27*(12), 39–41.

National Joint Committee on Learning Disabilities. (1985b). Learning disabilities: Issues on the preparation of professional personnel. *Asha, 27*(9), 49–51.

Note. The following National Joint Committee on Learning Disabilities papers were consulted for this paper, and can be found in this book:

"Learning Disabilities: Issues on Definition," 1981

"In-service Programs in Learning Disabilities," 1981

"Adults with Learning Disabilities: A Call to Action," 1985

"Learning Disabilities: Issues in the Preparation of Professional Personnel," 1982

The Need for Subject Descriptors in Learning Disabilities Research: Preschool Through High School Years

A Position Paper of the National Joint Committee on Learning Disabilities
September, 1989

RESEARCH ACTIVITIES IN THE AREA OF LEARNING DISABILITIES ARE extensive. The findings from these studies have influenced funding, program development, education, and treatment for individuals with learning disabilities. Research is based on the use of single subject, within subject, and group comparison models. Across studies there is inconsistency in the description of subjects. There is also inadequate information regarding subject selection and study methodology. These inconsistencies and omissions are of concern to the National Joint Committee on Learning Disabilities (NJCLD). Limited subject description makes it difficult to interpret and generalize research findings and interferes with replication studies.

The purpose of this paper is to provide a set of descriptors the NJCLD believes are necessary to describe subjects in studies of learning disabilities. Documentation of these descriptors will facilitate replication of research and application of findings by practitioners. This paper will provide guidance to funding agencies, investigators, university programs and other agencies that conduct or supervise research as well as to authors, editors, and publishers who disseminate research findings.

The need for specific subject descriptors in learning disabilities research is based on recognition of the following factors:

- the heterogeneity of learning disabilities necessitates a description of subjects included in a research study;

- many research studies include individuals classified as learning disabled on the basis of state or local service agency criteria, which vary among agencies;

- various procedures are used to determine ability, aptitude, and achievement.

The NJCLD recognizes that there may be problems collecting subject information as a result of factors such as study setting, e.g., school, clinic, hospital. These difficulties can limit the kinds and amount of subject information available. Therefore, the NJCLD recommends that investigators report all relevant facts related to the collection of subject information.

The NJCLD urges all investigators to document the criteria for subject inclusion as well as provide a description of all tests and experimental measures used in the study. To facilitate replication, consistency in research design, and reporting of subject information across studies, the following subject descriptors are recommended:

I. Demographic Data
   - Sample size
   - Gender
   - Socioeconomic status
   - Cultural/ethnic background
   - Dominant language dialect
   - Chronological age
   - Race
   - Maternal education
   - Locale: urban, suburban, rural
   - Geographic region

II. Health and Medical History
   - Medical, including neurological/developmental, history
   - Sensory System problems

III. Education Data
   - Grade placement
   - Educational history, including current educational setting
   - Related services provided
   - Curricular and instructional histories

IV. Characteristics at the Time of Study
   - Sensory and medical status at the time of the study
   - Intellectual level
   - Behavioral and emotional status
   - Receptive and expressive language abilities
   - Achievement levels

Professional Development Issues

Professional Development for Teachers

A Report from the
National Joint Committee
on Learning Disabilities
January 31, 1999

PROFESSIONAL DEVELOPMENT

During this time of educational reform, state boards of education and local school districts are setting high academic standards for all students, including students with learning disabilities. The 1997 reauthorization of the Individuals with Disabilities Education Act ensures the involvement of both general and special education teachers in the education of students with learning disabilities. This includes the development of individualized education programs that address the knowledge and skills needed by students with learning disabilities, so they can access the general education curriculum and participate in statewide and district wide assessments. If all students are to obtain high levels of achievement within more diverse classrooms, the message is clear: *Unless effective professional development is an integral part of a school district's strategic plan, it is unlikely to meet the learning needs of all students.*

PURPOSE

The purpose of this National Joint Committee on Learning Disabilities (NJCLD) paper is to support professional development, principles, and practices that ultimately result in high achievement for all students, especially students with learning disabilities. These principles and practices reflect agreement with and are based on standards developed by the National Staff Development Council (1995). NJCLD believes that professional development is no longer considered necessary for teachers only. Everyone who has an effect on student learning—from the members of boards of education, superintendents, administrators, and teachers to the support staff and parent/guardians—must continuously improve their knowledge, skills, and attitudes. Professional development is not the exclusive responsibility of someone given the title of staff developer, but rather the shared responsibility of all who are involved with students.

The teacher competencies critical to student achievement have changed significantly. To teach effectively, teachers must possess a rich understanding of pedagogical and content-specific knowledge (see the report "Learning Disabilities: Preservice Preparation of General and Special Education Teachers," 1997, in this book). Educational reform, increased knowledge of the teaching-learning process, and greater access to the general education curriculum for students with learning disabilities necessitate changes in professional development practice. Teachers must add to their instructional repertoire. Their instructional skills will only evolve if they learn new methods and approaches. They must demonstrate an extensive knowledge of practical strategies, and be accomplished in the skills needed to teach their students. Teacher and student learning must be interconnected.

At one time professional development was synonymous with "sit and get" sessions in which relatively passive participants were "made aware" of the latest ideas regarding teaching and learning from "experts." Today professional development must include high-quality, ongoing training that reflects a variety of approaches, with intensive follow-up and support. *NJCLD strongly believes that professional development is an ongoing process of continuous improvement that includes meaningful needs assessment, intensive informational sessions, and long term follow-up and support. It is not an event.*

PRINCIPLES FOR PROFESSIONAL DEVELOPMENT

Effective professional development programs are dynamic and integrated. They address the organizational, systemic, and cultural supports needed (the context); the way content-specific knowledge, pedagogy, skills, and attitudes are acquired (the process); and the content-specific knowledge, pedagogy, skills, and attitudes needed (the content). Continuous evaluation of student achievement, relative to high academic standards, must be a driving force in shaping professional development plans. The needs of the individual, groups of individuals, school(s), the school district, and the state's educational agency must also be addressed.

The Context

Effective continuous professional development:

- Supports the ongoing acquisition of new skills to ensure that all students, including students with learning disabilities, are involved and progress in the general curriculum.

Professional development should not be defined by several days of programs each school year. The very culture of the school must support continuous inquiry and reflection on the implementation and development of best practices. Protecting and nurturing research-based approaches will ensure that all students, including students with learning disabilities, will achieve in the general curriculum.

- Requires strong leadership, supported by the entire educational community, that encourages and provides staff with opportunities and resources to pursue the acquisition of new skills.

Effective professional development plans promote collaborative relationships, partnerships, increased parent involvement, and strong stakeholder support. State education agencies, school boards and administrators must encourage and provide opportunities, incentives, and resources for school staff to pursue ongoing and career-long learning. Knowledgeable school personnel facilitate high levels of learning, so all students achieve rigorous academic standards.

- Is adequately funded and is an integral part of the school's strategic plan.

Comprehensive professional development will be given genuine consideration and adequate funding only when it is an integral part of a school district's strategic plan. With this type of priority status, professional development is perceived by the entire district and community as a critical factor in the quest for excellence in student achievement.

- Provides sufficient time during the workday for staff members to learn and work together.

In its 1994 report "Prisoners of Time," the National Education Commission on Time and Learning indicated that school personnel need time to work with and learn from their colleagues. This time is necessary for individuals to master their disciplines, effectively use assessment systems, and design learning experiences for students that result in the achievement of high academic standards. This time is essential for the redefinition of an existing system which often defines a teacher's professional activity almost solely as the time spent in front of students, dooming both students and teachers to failure.

- Requires an understanding of the change process.

Systemic change inherently includes the reexamination of beliefs and assumptions about professional development. Understanding that the process of change cannot be mandated, takes time, and may be uncomfortable better prepares districts for successful reform. This change process must be supported and sustained through policy and sufficient funding so it becomes an integral component of the district's mission.

The Process

Effective continuous professional development:

- Is based on the principles of adult learning.

Effective models of professional development reflect current knowledge of adult learning. Adults need to know that their efforts will result in increased achievement by their students. Adults are motivated to learn when professional development provides opportunity to achieve competency, combines independent and dependent approaches, has clear and measurable outcomes, and respects their intellectual potential and capability.

- Provides for the three phases of the change process: initiation, implementation, and institutionalization.

Change must be considered as a process not an event. Professional development planning must address the three critical phases of this process: initiation, implementation, and institutionalization (Fullan, 1991). During initiation a clear need to improve is established. In the second phase, implementation, a plan that addresses knowledge, skills, and attitudes is developed, implemented, and monitored. Lastly, during institutionalization, organizational structures support and sustain the initiatives, so they become an integral component of effective practice.

- Provides a variety of approaches that may include these models: study groups, teacher research, peer coaching, portfolio development, individually guided professional development, observation/assessment, involvement in a development/improvement process, training, and inquiry.

Effective professional development plans appropriately use a variety of approaches to help achieve the goals of high standards for teacher and student learning. The National Staff Development Council (1995) has noted that the characteristics of a productive professional development program include:

- *Connectedness to school settings and to school wide efforts*
- *Involvement of school personnel as planners*
- *Providing choice and differentiated learning opportunities*
- *Use of demonstration, supervised practice, and feedback as a part of training*
- *Ongoing assistance and support*

- Provides planned follow-up that includes peer coaching, collegial support groups, mentoring, and study groups designed to ensure effective implementation.

Research shows that implementation and institutionalization of new skills and knowledge do not occur without planned follow-up. These opportunities for practice of new skills allow school personnel to increase student achievement by focusing and reflecting on their performance, the efficacy of ongoing professional development, and the impact on student outcomes.

- Provides staff with the collaborative skills needed to make decisions, solve problems, and work together.

High quality, professional development plans and programs are developed collaboratively by those who will implement and institutionalize them. Empowering school personnel in the process promotes greater ownership for the achievement of all students including students with learning disabilities. To create a collaborative workplace, school personnel must practice respectful listening, be open minded to others' perspectives, support risk taking, and maintain professional confidentiality.

- Requires an ongoing evaluation of the use and effectiveness of the plan, which includes multiple sources of information and focuses at all levels of the educational community.

Evaluation is an integral component of any professional development plan. Assessment of participant reaction, learning, uses of knowledge and skills, and impact on student learning and achievement should be analyzed to determine effectiveness of the plan. Both formative and summative evaluation methods should be used to collect information. High quality professional development must ultimately be evaluated on the basis of school personnel effectiveness and student-demonstrated knowledge and skill.

The Content

Effective continuous professional development:

- Increases the understanding of how to create school environments and provide instruction that is responsive to the diverse and developmental needs of students, including students with learning disabilities.

The National Center to Improve the Tools of Educators (NCITE) has identified six features of instruction that efficiently accommodate and accelerate student learning.

Big ideas—concepts and principles that facilitate the most efficient and broadest acquisition of knowledge across a range of examples.

Conspicuous strategies—strategies which are an approximation of the steps experts follow covertly to solve complex problems and difficult tasks.

Primed background knowledge—before the understanding of new information can occur, necessary background knowledge must be taught or "primed." This requires teaching component steps and concepts that allow an in-depth understanding of a big idea or strategy.

Mediated scaffolding—refers to the guidance, assistance, and support that a teacher, peer or task provides to a learner.

Judicious review—should be (a) sufficient for initial learning to occur, (b) distributed over time, (c) varied for generalizability, and (d) cumulative.

Strategic integration—the process whereby prior learning is integrated into more complex concepts.

- Prepares teachers in the effective use of appropriate academic modifications and accommodations.

In order to provide access to the general education curriculum, school personnel who work with students with learning disabilities must be knowledgeable of and provide appropriate accommodations and modifications in instruction and assessment. Successful implementation and continuous evaluation of these will allow students to participate and progress in the general education curriculum. This knowledge base will also facilitate effective participation by school personnel in the development of individualized educational programs.

- Facilitates the development and implementation of positive school climate, classroom management, services, and strategies to maximize student learning.

School personnel who work with students with learning disabilities are responsible for the development and implementation of positive school climate, classroom management, services, and strategies to maximize success.

Positive attitudes and perceptions about learning are key elements of effective instruction, particularly for students with learning disabilities. Teachers must use strategies that create a positive learning climate in which students feel that they are capable of learning, encouraged to engage in the learning process, recognized for their contributions, and provided assistance for success.

Classroom management is a critical competency for all teachers and often a focus of professional development for beginning educators. It is particularly important that educators who

NOTES

work with students with learning disabilities must create and articulate rules and procedures that convey a sense of direction, order and meaningfulness for learning.

School personnel must understand the continuum of services and placements for students with learning disabilities and their role in the decision making process and/or implementation of delivery of services within the educational setting.

It is critical that educators of students with learning disabilities have a working knowledge base of strategies that facilitate student learning. These include both instructional and student strategies for the acquisition, organization, and expression of knowledge.

- Enables teachers to use a variety of research-based instructional approaches appropriately to meet the needs of their students, including academic skills and learning and organizational strategies for students with learning disabilities.

To empower students to benefit from their classroom experiences, educators must possess the tools necessary to deliver effective instruction appropriate to the level of the student to ensure success. They must have the competencies for effective teaching of students with learning disabilities at all levels of severity. Research-based instructional tools must be disseminated to professional development providers, who in turn must incorporate these proven practices into training curricula. Serious efforts must be made by state education agencies to make information about these tools and practices available to both teacher preparation programs and local schools, who must be given the time and opportunities to institutionalize these practices.

- Facilitates collaboration among staff, families, and community in order to improve student performance.

Effective ongoing professional development helps school personnel learn to collaborate among themselves as well as with the community at large. The entire community must be invested in the success of all students. Schools that nurture the relationships among staff, families, and community have the best opportunities for successful implementation of effective learning experiences for all students, including those with learning disabilities. All stakeholders must embrace the notion of true collaboration for success, if the goal of high academic standards and achievement for all students including those with learning disabilities is to be realized.

- Prepares teachers to effectively use various performance assessments in their classrooms to measure the progress of all students, including students with learning disabilities.

In order for students to demonstrate progress in achieving high academic standards, school personnel must be able to effectively use various performance assessments within the educational setting. While one student may be able to demonstrate skills and knowledge using paper and pencil tests, another may not, due to his/her disability, yet still have the same level of competency. Given that it is critical for educators to be able to use various instructional strategies and techniques to meet the needs of diverse learners, it is essential for them to have a repertoire of tools to assess the competencies of these learners.

- Prepares teachers to meet the needs of students with learning disabilities through the use of technology across the curriculum.

Technology is an important tool for both instruction and learning. Educators must have a working knowledge of technology-based programs that can be used to enhance, extend, and supplement instruction. Also, educators must be aware of technology that assists students, especially those with learning disabilities, in accessing curriculum, such as taped materials, graphic organizers, and computer-enhanced text. In addition, educators should be knowledgeable of and, when appropriate, use technologies that allow students to demonstrate their skills and knowledge, such as word processing, voice recognition and text-to-speech software.

- Prepares teachers to provide instruction to students with learning disabilities in social skills, life skills, self-advocacy, and preparation for transitions.

School personnel need the skills to provide students with learning disabilities instruction in social skills, self-regulatory behaviors, life skills, and self-advocacy, and to prepare them for transition. While it is important for these students to achieve high academic standards, it is critical for them to develop social competency and to prepare for a successful life beyond high school.

SUMMARY

NJCLD recognizes that school improvement for all students, including students with learning disabilities, is a systemic process, and that changes in one part of the system will require changes in other parts of the system. The above principles for effective continuous professional development reflect agreement with the standards developed by the National Staff Development Council (1995).

NOTES

Professional development both influences and is influenced by the organizational context in which it takes place. Continuous evaluation of student achievement relative to high academic standards, and evaluation of progress toward successful independence as a student and employee, and ability to become an effective self-advocate within educational, vocational, and social realms must be a driving force in modifying current plans and shaping future professional development plans. This can best be accomplished through professional development that is consistent with National Staff Development Council standards, is an ongoing, need-driven process, and includes both strong expert sessions and effective support and follow-up. Professional development plans must address the needs of the individual, groups of individuals, school(s), school districts, and state educational agencies to achieve the goals of education. *Effective professional development is an ongoing process, not an event.*

REFERENCES

Fullan, M. G. (1991). *The new meaning of educational change.* New York: Teachers College Press.

Individuals with Disabilities Education Act Amendments of 1997, 20 U.S.C. § 14 *et seq.*

National Education Commission on Time and Learning. (1994). *Prisoners of time.* Washington, DC: Government Printing Office.

Note. The following National Joint Committee on Learning Disabilities paper and report were cited in or consulted for this report, and can be found in this book:

"In-service Programs in Learning Disabilities," 1981

"Learning Disabilities: Preservice Preparation of General and Special Education Teachers," 1997

Other sources consulted:

Standards for Staff Development: Elementary School Level, 1995, and *Standards for Staff Development: High School Level,* 1995, by National Staff Development Council and National Association of Secondary School Principals, Oxford, OH and Alexandria, VA: Author.

Learning Disabilities: Use of Paraprofessionals

**A Report from the
National Joint Committee
on Learning Disabilities
February 1, 1998**

INTRODUCTION

Since its inception, the Individuals with Disabilities Education Act (IDEA) has embodied the concept of teams of professionals, often from different disciplines, working together to meet the needs of children and youth with disabilities and their families. In recent years the team concept has expanded to include paraprofessionals as members of these teams. The term "paraprofessional" is used in IDEA [Sec. 612(a)(15)(B)(iii)]. The term "paraprofessional" is used in this document as an inclusive term applying to a group of resources and job titles (see the definition of paraprofessionals on p. 80).

Paraprofessionals are employees who, following appropriate academic education/instruction and/or on-the-job training, perform tasks as prescribed, directed, and supervised by qualified professionals such as general education teachers, resource teachers, self-contained class teachers, reading teachers, learning disability specialists; speech-language pathologists, school psychologists, occupational therapists, physical therapists, and other instruction, special education, and related service personnel.

The intent of using paraprofessionals is to supplement not supplant the work of the teacher/service provider. Paraprofessionals can assist in providing a variety of activities based on their training and scope of responsibilities. Paraprofessionals can be used to increase the frequency, intensity, efficiency, and availability of instructional assistance and services as delegated and supervised by the qualified teacher/service provider; they can assist the qualified supervising teacher/service provider with generalization of learned skills to multiple settings; and they can assist with habilitation and education programs. The use of paraprofessionals can increase access to services for diverse and underserved populations. Paraprofessionals often are drawn from the surrounding community and may provide a link to families that are culturally and linguistically diverse. The use of well-trained and supervised paraprofessionals is one way to increase the frequency of services while maintaining the quality of services provided.

> *Note:* NJCLD member associations and organizations that have approved this document may have standards, positions, guidelines, and other policies related specifically to the use and supervision of paraprofessionals, support personnel, or assistants. Members of the associations and organizations listed as approving this document should contact

their association or organization for additional information that may determine how they should use and supervise paraprofessionals, support personnel, or assistants.

As professional roles expand there is a growing appreciation for paraprofessionals who can perform a diverse array of tasks. Although awareness of the potential of paraprofessionals is growing, there is equal concern for ensuring that paraprofessionals are used appropriately and that they receive adequate training and supervision for the roles and responsibilities they assume. Although some states and some organizations have begun to articulate standards or guidelines concerning the use of paraprofessionals, there is wide variance in the roles and standards in use to date. As policies and procedures for the use of paraprofessionals are developed, it is important to ensure that both quality of service and access to service are maintained for all those in need of service. The decision to shift responsibility for implementation of the more repetitive, mechanical, or routine instructional activities to paraprofessionals should be made only by fully qualified professionals and when the quality of service and level of professionalism will not be compromised. Professional judgment should be at the heart of the selection, management, supervision, and use of paraprofessionals.

When using paraprofessionals in programs serving individuals with learning disabilities, it is important to remember that consumers have a right to know who is providing the service (i.e., by a professional or by a paraprofessional). Teachers/service providers must inform consumers when services are provided by paraprofessionals. Qualified teachers/service providers may delegate certain tasks to paraprofessionals, but the professionals retain the legal and ethical responsibility for all services provided or omitted. Use of paraprofessionals is an appropriate option in educational agencies, particularly when supported by state standards and licensure laws, local policies, procedures, and administrative support. Teachers/service providers should never be required to use paraprofessionals, particularly if they feel that quality of service may be compromised.

The purpose of this document is to provide a framework for use by education agencies in developing rules and guidelines for use of paraprofessionals within programs serving individuals with learning disabilities; by postsecondary institutions and related agencies in developing education and professional development programs; and by administrators and teachers/service providers responsible for developing comprehensive systems of services.

FOUNDATION FOR SUCCESSFUL PARAPROFESSIONAL SERVICES

The foundation for successfully using a paraprofessional service delivery model includes:

1. Administrative understanding of the benefits and restrictions of using paraprofessionals.

2. Availability of qualified teachers/service providers with an understanding and commitment to the training, use, and supervision of paraprofessionals.

3. Provision of sufficient resources and empowerment of teachers/service providers to decide whether to use paraprofessionals.

4. Provision of sufficient time for teachers/service providers to adequately train and supervise paraprofessionals.

5. Availability of qualified people to work as paraprofessionals.

6. Sufficient education for all personnel on the role, use, and supervision of paraprofessionals.

7. Availability of ongoing and appropriate professional development programs for paraprofessionals used in programs serving individuals with learning disabilities.

It must be stressed that the optional use of paraprofessionals in programs for individuals with learning disabilities must not preclude active recruitment of qualified teachers/service providers who can meet the full requirements for state certification/licensure.

KEY WORD DEFINITIONS

Paraprofessionals

Paraprofessionals are employees who, following appropriate academic education/instruction and/or on-the-job training, perform tasks as prescribed, directed, and supervised by fully qualified professionals. Job titles for paraprofessionals may include terms such as "aide," "assistant," "associate," "para-educator," "instructional assistant," and "classroom aide," among others. The intent of using paraprofessionals is to supplement not supplant the work of the teacher/service provider.

Teacher/Service Provider

Teachers/service providers include qualified professionals such as general education teachers, resource teachers, self-contained class teachers, reading teachers, learning disability specialists, speech-language pathologists, school psychologists, occupational therapists, physical therapists, and other instruction, special education, and related service personnel.

Qualified Professional

A qualified professional is an individual who meets the highest requirements in the state for employment in his or her area of expertise, is certified or licensed by the appropriate state authority, and, if required, is credentialed by the nationally recognized, reliable certification authority for that profession.

Direct Supervision

Direct supervision means on-site, in-view observation and guidance by a qualified teacher/service provider while paraprofessionals perform an assigned activity.

Indirect Supervision

Indirect supervision means those activities other than direct observation and guidance conducted by a qualified teacher/service provider that may include demonstration, record review, review and evaluation of audio or videotaped sessions, and/or interactive television.

Individual Plan

This terminology is meant to include, but not be limited to, the "Individualized Education Program (IEP)," "Individualized Family Service Plan (IFSP)," "Individual Transition Plan," and other plans that outline the services to be provided to an individual with a learning disability.

ETHICAL RESPONSIBILITIES

It is imperative that teachers/service providers who supervise paraprofessionals consider the code of ethics in their profession. The consumer must be informed about the use of paraprofessionals. The supervising teacher/service provider and paraprofessional must exercise caution to avoid misrepresentation by implying that the individual serving as a paraprofessional is a qualified professional.

Paraprofessionals are a complement for, rather than an alternative to, professional service. Paraprofessionals must not provide service without supervision of an appropriately qualified professional. As a supervisor, the teacher/service provider has direct responsibility for correction of inappropriate actions by paraprofessionals. Supervisors who fail to provide appropriate supervision of paraprofessionals may be in violation of their profession's code of ethics.

EDUCATION REQUIREMENTS FOR PARAPROFESSIONALS

The education requirements for paraprofessionals vary depending on the activities they will be required to carry out and the roles and responsibilities for paraprofessionals. For example, paraprofessionals who will provide clerical duties and have minimal direct contact with students would require a high school degree, GED, or equivalent training and experience. Paraprofessionals who are expected to complete higher level activities and have increased direct contact with students may be required to have an associate's degree or higher in an educationally related field from a state-approved and -accredited postsecondary program. Regardless of their education, paraprofessionals must be supervised by a teacher/service provider who meets the highest requirements in the state for employment in his or her area of expertise, is certified or licensed by the appropriate state authority, and, if required, is credentialed by the nationally recognized, reliable certification authority for that profession.

Responsibilities for paraprofessionals used in programs serving individuals with learning disabilities may be designated to an individual:

1. who meets the expected educational requirements;
2. who demonstrates proficiency in skills required for paraprofessionals;

3. who is supervised by a qualified teacher/service provider;
4. who adheres to applicable state certification, registration or licensure laws, and rules regulating the use of paraprofessionals.

Note. See Appendix A for a list of recommended competencies for paraprofessionals and Appendix B for a list of recommended competencies for the supervising teacher/service provider.

ROLES AND RESPONSIBILITIES OF PARAPROFESSIONALS IN A LEARNING DISABILITIES PROGRAM

Although the teacher/service provider may delegate specific tasks to a paraprofessional, the legal (e.g., professional liability) and ethical responsibility to the student for all services provided or omitted cannot be delegated. These must remain the full responsibility of the supervising teacher/service provider. A paraprofessional may execute specific components of a program as specified in an individualized plan under the direction and supervision of a qualified teacher/service provider. Tasks to be executed by the paraprofessional are only those that are within the scope of responsibilities for paraprofessionals and are tasks that the supervising teacher/service provider has determined the paraprofessional has the training and expertise to perform. The teacher/service provider must provide at least the minimum specified level of supervision to ensure quality of services to all persons served. The amount of supervision may vary and must depend on the complexity of the student's disability and individual plan and the experience of the paraprofessional. The educational agency must maintain documentation of preservice training, in-service training, and supervision of the paraprofessional.

Provided that the training and supervision are appropriate, the following general tasks may be delegated to an entry-level paraprofessional used in programs serving individuals with learning disabilities. Individuals who have a high school degree, GED, or equivalent training and experience may do the following:

a. Assist with informal documentation (e.g., tallying notes for the teacher/service provider to use), prepare materials, and assist with other clerical duties as directed by the supervising teacher/service provider.

b. Schedule activities, prepare charts, records, graphs, or otherwise display data.

c. Perform checks and maintenance of equipment.

d. Implement, under the direct supervision of the qualified supervising teacher or teacher/service provider, supplemental instructional assistance activities.

The paraprofessional who has an associate's degree or higher from a state-approved and -accredited postsecondary program, or equivalent training and experience may do the following higher level activities to supplement the work of the qualified teacher/service provider:

a. Conduct screenings (without interpretation) following specified screening protocols developed by the qualified supervising teacher/service provider.

b. Assist in providing supplementary work and reinforce learning in small groups or with individuals while the teacher/service provider works with other individuals.

c. Record student progress toward meeting established objectives as stated in the individualized plan, and report this information to the supervising teacher/service provider.

d. Provide direct supplemental instruction/intervention services included in the individualized plans as identified and directed by the supervising teacher/service provider.

e. Use positive behavior supports consistent with those used by the supervising teacher/service provider.

f. Assist the teacher/service provider during assessment of students, such as those who are difficult to test.

g. Participate with the teacher/service provider in research projects, in-service training, and public relations programs.

Specific job activities for a paraprofessional are to be determined by the supervising teacher/service provider based on the education and experience of the individual. The paraprofessional with more education and more years of successful experience may be asked to carry out more complex activities.

ACTIVITIES OUTSIDE THE SCOPE OF RESPONSIBILITIES FOR PARAPROFESSIONALS

There is a potential for misuse of paraprofessionals, particularly when responsibilities are delegated by other staff without the knowledge and approval of the supervising teacher/service provider. Therefore, the paraprofessional should not be placed in a position to perform any task without the express knowledge and approval of the supervising teacher/service provider. Paraprofessionals used in programs serving individuals with learning disabilities shall not:

a. Be solely responsible for instruction or provision of professional services.

b. Perform or interpret standardized or nonstandardized assessments, formal or informal, unless specifically trained to provide such tests and evaluations and supervised by the qualified teacher/service provider.

c. Participate in parent conferences, student conferences, or any interdisciplinary teams in place of the supervising teacher/service provider.

d. Communicate with the individual with learning disabilities, family, or others regarding any aspect of the student's status or service without the specific consent of the supervising teacher/service provider or provide student or family counseling.

e. Write, develop, or modify an individualized plan in any way or assist with instruction/intervention without following the individual plan prepared under the direction of the teacher/service provider or without access to supervision.

f. Sign any formal documents (e.g., individual plans, service reimbursement forms, or reports) as a substitute for the qualified professional. Paraprofessionals should sign or initial informal progress notes for review and co-signature by the supervising teacher/service provider.

g. Select individuals for services, make referrals for additional services, assign grades, or discharge an individual from service.

NOTES

h. Disclose educational, clinical, or confidential information either orally or in writing to anyone not designated by the supervising teacher/service provider.

i. Represent himself or herself as a qualified teacher/service provider or be used as a substitute for a qualified teacher/service provider unless he/she possesses the appropriate certification/licensure to function as a substitute and is hired as a substitute.

RESPONSIBILITIES OF THE QUALIFIED TEACHER/SERVICE PROVIDER WITH REGARD TO USE OF PARAPROFESSIONALS

For effective use of a paraprofessional, the supervising teacher/service provider should:

1. Participate in supervision training prior to using a paraprofessional and upgrade supervision knowledge and skills on a regular basis.

2. Participate significantly in hiring of the paraprofessional for which they will be responsible.

3. Inform the family and student about the level (professional vs. paraprofessional), frequency, and duration of services as well as the extent of supervision.

4. Review each individual plan with the paraprofessional at least weekly.

5. Delegate specific tasks to the paraprofessional while retaining legal and ethical responsibility for all services provided or omitted.

6. Sign all formal documents (e.g., individual plans, reports). The supervisor should indicate on documents that the paraprofessional performed certain activities.

7. Review and sign all informal progress notes prepared by the paraprofessional.

8. Provide ongoing on-the-job training for the paraprofessional.

9. Provide and document appropriate supervision of the paraprofessional.

10. Ensure that the paraprofessional only performs tasks within the scope of responsibility for the paraprofessional.

11. Participate in the performance appraisal of the paraprofessional for which they are responsible.

GUIDELINES FOR SUPERVISION OF PARAPROFESSIONALS

It is the responsibility of the teacher/service provider to design and implement a supervision system that maintains the highest possible standards of quality. The amount and type of supervision required should be based on the skills and experience of the paraprofessional, the needs of students served, the service setting, the tasks assigned, and other factors. More intense supervision, for example, would be required in such instances as the initial work of a new paraprofessional; initiation of a new program, equipment, or task; or a change in the student's status (e.g., educational, medical, personal complications).

Paraprofessionals must be supervised by a qualified teacher/service provider who meets the highest requirements in the state for employment in his or her area of expertise, is certified or licensed by the appropriate state authority, and, if required, is credentialed by the nationally recognized, reliable certification authority for that profession.

In addition, completion of at least one academic course or continuing education unit in supervision is highly desired. Periodic updating of supervision skills through professional development is the responsibility of the teacher/service provider. Because the supervision process is such a close, interpersonal experience, the supervising teacher/service provider should participate in the selection of paraprofessionals used in programs serving individuals with learning disabilities.

Supervision by Qualified Classroom Teachers

In the classroom, the teacher supervises a paraprofessional on a daily, or regularly scheduled, basis. This can be accomplished in different ways (direct and indirect) depending on the duties of the paraprofessional and the organization of the classroom. The teacher, through frequent modeling and coaching, can guide the paraprofessional toward increased competency in working with students who have learning disabilities.

Teachers need to directly supervise a paraprofessional on a more intensive basis in the initial stages of material preparation, lesson presentation, instructional assistance, guided practice, group process, classroom management, behavior management, and other student interactions. As the paraprofessional becomes more proficient in carrying out assigned tasks, the teacher can vary the nature and extent of supervision. Allowing provision of instructional assistance or services to students with learning disabilities by the paraprofessional without a qualified teacher in view is always determined by the policy of the employing educational agency.

Ideally, the classroom teacher and the paraprofessional work as a team, rather than independent instructors, to assist student learning. Supervision is designed to bring the teacher and the paraprofessional closer to that team concept, and increase the skills of both in meeting the needs of students with learning disabilities.

Supervision by Qualified Service Providers

As a minimum, supervision of paraprofessionals should be completed according to the following schedule:

a. The first 10 hours of direct contact with the individual with learning disabilities following training.

b. Ten percent (10%) of all instruction/intervention sessions after the first 10 hours of student contact including at least one in every ten consecutive sessions.

c. After the initial 10 hours of direct supervision, the amount of supervision may be adjusted depending on the competency of the paraprofessional, the needs of the students served, and the nature of the assigned tasks. The minimum is 10% direct supervision.

The supervision plan developed by the supervising teacher/service provider and the paraprofessional must ensure that the supervisor will have direct contact time with the paraprofessional as well as with the individuals served by the paraprofessional. During each week, data on every individual seen by the paraprofessional must be reviewed by the supervisor. In addition, direct supervision should be scheduled so that all individuals seen by the paraprofessional are directly supervised by the teacher/service provider at least once every two weeks. Supervision days and time of day (morning/afternoon) may be alternated to ensure that all individuals receive some direct contact with the teacher/service provider at least once every two weeks. Direct supervision means on-site, in-view observation and guidance while an activity is performed.

Supervision should provide information about the quality of the paraprofessional's performance of assigned tasks and should verify that instructional/clinical activity is limited to tasks specified in the paraprofessional's scope of responsibilities. Information obtained during direct supervision may include data relative to (a) agreement (reliability) between the paraprofessional and the supervisor on correct/incorrect recording of target behavior, (b) accuracy in implementation of screening and instructional/clinical procedures, (c) accuracy in recording data, and (d) ability to interact effectively with the student.

In addition to direct supervision, indirect supervision is required and may include demonstration, record review, review and evaluation of audio or videotaped sessions, interactive television, and/or supervisory conferences that may be conducted by telephone. Additional direct and indirect supervision, beyond the minimum required, may be necessary depending on the skills of the paraprofessional and the needs of the students with learning disabilities being served. Functional assessment of the paraprofessional's skills with assigned tasks should be an ongoing, integral element of supervision necessary to determine the adequate and appropriate amount of supervision that must be provided.

At no time may a paraprofessional perform tasks when a supervising teacher/service provider cannot be reached by personal contact, phone, pager, or other immediate means. If for any reason (i.e., maternity leave, illness, change of jobs) the supervisor is no longer available to provide the level of supervision stipulated, the paraprofessional may not perform tasks until a fully qualified teacher/service provider has been designated as the paraprofessional's supervisor.

Although more than one teacher/service provider may provide supervision for an individual serving as a paraprofessional, at no time may a teacher/service provider supervise or be listed as a supervisor for more than three (3) paraprofessionals. The supervising teacher/service provider should be the only professional to decide the number of paraprofessionals to use (i.e., 0, 1, 2, or 3). When multiple supervisors are used for one paraprofessional, the supervisors are encouraged to coordinate and communicate with each other.

CONCLUSION

Paraprofessionals used in programs that serve individuals with learning disabilities may be used to supplement, enhance, and extend programs and services not supplant them. The purpose of using paraprofessionals is not to increase the class/caseload size for teachers/service providers. Rather it is to increase the frequency, intensity, and appropriateness of services so that a greater number of students have the opportunity to experience and achieve academic success. The use of appropriately trained and supervised paraprofessionals is seen as a mechanism to achieve effective service outcomes within a cost-effective system of quality service delivery. There is a critical need for all programs that use paraprofessionals to adhere to these recommendations for use of paraprofessionals to ensure the provision of high quality services, use of well-prepared qualified professionals and paraprofessionals, effective supervision, and coordinated service delivery by the qualified teacher/service provider and paraprofessional team.

REFERENCE

Individuals with Disabilities Education Act of 1990, 20 U.S.C. § 1400 *et seq.*

Note. The following sources were consulted in the preparation of this report:

"Guidelines for the Training, Credentialing, Use, and Supervision of Speech–Language Pathology Assistants," by American Speech-Language-Hearing Association, 1996, *Asha, 38,* (Suppl. 16), p. 21–34.

Report of the Consortium of Organizations on the Preparation and Use of Speech–Language Paraprofessionals in Early Intervention and Education Settings, by Council for Exceptional Children, 1997, Reston, VA: Author.

Organizations participating in the Consortium:

American Speech-Language-Hearing Association (ASHA)

Council for Exceptional Children (CEC)

Council of Administrators of Special Education (CASE)

Council of Language, Speech, and Hearing Consultants in State Education Agencies (CLSHCSEA)

Division for Children's Communication Development (DCCD)

Division for Early Childhood (DEC)

Appendix A: Recommended Competencies for Paraprofessionals

FOLLOWING ARE BASIC COMPETENCIES NEEDED BY PARAPROfessionals used in programs serving individuals with learning disabilities:

I. INTERPERSONAL SKILLS (Communicates honestly, clearly, accurately, coherently, and concisely.)

1. Deals effectively with attitudes and behaviors of the individual with learning disabilities.

    a. Maintains appropriate relationships

    b. Is sensitive to the cultural values of the student and family

    c. Takes into proper consideration the individual's strengths and needs

    d. Demonstrates an appropriate level of self-confidence when performing assigned tasks

    e. Demonstrates insight in attitudes and behaviors

    f. Directs the individual, family, and professionals to supervisor for information regarding testing, services, and referral

2. Uses appropriate language (written and oral) in dealing with the individual with learning disabilities and others

    a. Uses language appropriate for the individual's and other's age and educational level

    b. Is courteous and respectful at all times

    c. Maintains appropriate social interaction

3. Deals effectively with supervisor

    a. Is receptive to constructive criticism

    b. Requests assistance from supervisor as needed

c. Actively participates in interaction with supervisor

II. PERSONAL QUALITIES

1. Manages time effectively

   a. Arrives punctually and prepared for appointments

   b. Arrives punctually for work-related meetings (e.g., meetings with supervisor, staff, etc.)

   c. Turns in all documentation on time

2. Demonstrates appropriate conduct

   a. Respects/maintains confidentiality of the individual and family

   b. Maintains personal appearance appropriate for the work setting

   c. Uses appropriate language for the work setting

   d. Evaluates own performance

   e. Recognizes own professional limitations and performs within boundaries of training and job responsibilities

III. TECHNICAL SKILLS

1. Maintains a facilitating environment for assigned tasks

   a. Adjusts lighting and controls noise level

   b. Organizes work space

2. Uses time effectively

   a. Performs assigned tasks with no unnecessary distractions

   b. Completes assigned tasks within designated time

3. Prepares and presents materials effectively

   a. Selects materials ahead of time

   b. Uses appropriate materials based on the individual plan

   c. Prepares work setting to meet the needs of the individual for obtaining optimal performance

   d. Uses materials that are age- and culturally appropriate as well as motivating

4. Maintains records

   a. Records intervention activities and protocols accurately and concisely for supervisors

b. Reports the individual's performance to supervisor

c. Signs documents only when reviewed and co-signed by the supervisor

d. Prepares and maintains the individual's charts, records, and graphs for displaying data

5. Provides assistance to the teacher/service provider

   a. Assists the teacher/service provider during student assessment

   b. Assists with informal documentation

   c. Schedules activities

   d. Participates with the teacher/service provider in research projects

   e. Participates in professional development activities

   f. Participates with the teacher/service provider in public relations programs

IV. SCREENING (If an appropriate activity for the profession where paraprofessionals are used)

1. Demonstrates knowledge and use of a variety of screening tools and protocols

   a. Completes training on screening procedures

   b. Uses 2 to 3 screening instruments reliably

2. Demonstrates appropriate administration and scoring of screening tools

   a. Differentiates correct versus incorrect responses

   b. Completes (fills out) screening protocols accurately

   c. Scores screening instruments accurately

3. Manages screenings and documentation

   a. Reports any difficulty encountered in screening

   b. Schedules screenings

   c. Organizes screening materials

4. Communicates screening results and all supplemental information to supervisor for interpretation and decision-making

   a. Seeks supervisor's guidance when adaptation of screening tools and administration is in question

NOTES

b. Provides descriptive behavioral observations that contribute to screening results

V. INSTRUCTIONAL ASSISTANCE/INTERVENTION

1. Performs tasks as outlined and instructed by the supervisor

   a. Implements accurately and efficiently activities using procedures planned by the supervisor

   b. Uses constructive feedback from the supervisor for modifying interaction (interpersonal or otherwise) with the student

2. Demonstrates skills in managing behavior and intervention program

   a. Maintains on-task behavior

   b. Provides appropriate feedback as to the accuracy of the individual's response

   c. Uses feedback and reinforcement that are consistent, discriminating, and meaningful to the individual

   d. Gives directions and instructions that are clear, concise, and appropriate to the individual's age level and level of understanding

   e. Applies knowledge of behavior management during interaction with the individual

   f. Implements designated intervention goals/objectives in specified sequence

3. Demonstrates knowledge of education/intervention objectives and individual plan

   a. Demonstrates understanding of the individual's education/intervention needs

   b. Identifies correct versus incorrect responses

   c. Describes behaviors demonstrating a knowledge of the individual's overall level of progress

   d. Verbally reports and provides appropriate documentation of assigned activities to the supervising teacher/service provider

Appendix B: Recommended Competencies for the Qualified Supervising Teacher/Service Provider

THE SUPERVISING TEACHERS/SERVICE PROVIDERS ARE QUALIFIED professionals who meet the highest requirements in the state for employment in their specialty area. They will have acquired the knowledge, skills, and competencies needed to provide programs and services in their specialty area by meeting the academic and practicum requirements for obtaining certification or licensure as required by the state for their profession.

This document cannot list all of the clinical and programmatic knowledge and competencies needed by the supervising teachers/service providers for the numerous professions. However, the following are competencies needed by teachers/service providers who will be responsible for supervising paraprofessionals.

I. Interviewing skills

II. Mentoring

    1. Identifies and clarifies the roles and responsibilities of paraprofessionals

    2. Delineates lines of authority

    3. Demonstrates/models behavior

III. Communication

    1. Applies interpersonal skills

    2. Demonstrates elective listening skills

    3. Uses team-building skills

    4. Exhibits elective written and oral skills to provide team management

IV. Problem solving

    1. Resolves conflicts

    2. Identifies and clarifies a problem

    3. Assumes the perspective of another

V. Motivation skills

    1. Creates a positive environment

    2. Sets achievable goals

NOTES

3. Rewards goal achievement

4. Shows respect and acknowledges achievement of others

5. Promotes change and growth

VI. Coordination skills

1. Demonstrates time-management skills

2. Designs effective meeting strategies

3. Implements scheduling techniques

VII. Delegation skills

1. Selects tasks to be delegated based on an individual's competence

2. Clarifies roles and clearly delegates responsibilities

3. Provides constructive feedback to the delegate

VIII. Feedback and Evaluation skills

1. Monitors the performance of others

2. Provides constructive feedback

3. Participates in formal evaluation process

4. Describes and clarifies the evaluation process and content

5. Participates in individual personnel growth plans

Learning Disabilities: Preservice Preparation of General and Special Education Teachers

A Report from the
National Joint Committee
on Learning Disabilities
February 1, 1997

In memory of William Ellis, who initiated the National Joint Committee on Learning Disabilities' exploration of teacher preparation. Mr. Ellis served as a representative to the NJCLD for The Orton Dyslexia Society and the National Center for Learning Disabilities.

NOTES

THE NATIONAL JOINT COMMITTEE ON LEARNING DISABILITIES (NJCLD) believes it is essential that educators be prepared to meet the needs of all students, including students with learning disabilities who have unique needs. The NJCLD believes that comprehensive, interdisciplinary programs are necessary to ensure adequate preparation of professionals in education. Only then will there be the healthy exchange of ideas that will lead to a more complete view of how individuals learn. An interdisciplinary approach promotes the development and use of a core body of knowledge about human development, learning theory, language acquisition and disorders, and cultural and linguistic diversity, as well as relevant knowledge, skills, attitudes, values, and methods of associated disciplines. The purpose of this report is to identify the core competencies that the NJCLD believes are essential for both general and special educators who work with children with learning disabilities. The first part of the paper delineates competencies for general education teachers. The second part delineates additional competencies needed by special education teachers. Although these competencies represent the ideal, we believe they are worthy goals toward which every teacher preparation program should strive as it undergoes program review.

PREPARATION OF GENERAL EDUCATION TEACHERS IN A CORE CURRICULUM

All prospective teachers need to have, at a minimum, an overview of the scope and sequence of the curriculum from kindergarten through 12th grade. In addition, teachers should be well prepared in their subject areas and understand the central concepts and tools of inquiry in these areas.

The curricular areas required for all prospective teachers are reading, writing, communication skills, mathematics, social studies, the sciences, health/physical education, fine arts, and vocational/transition education. The emphasis in *early childhood* is on sensorimotor and social/emotional development, listening and speaking, and emerging reading, writing, and mathematical skills. In *elementary grades* the emphasis is on teaching and learning in reading, writing, and mathematics. During *middle school* the shift to classes by content area requires that children develop higher-level cognitive skills and understand the underlying concepts. Work on reading, writing, and reasoning within specific content areas throughout *middle and high school* is necessary. Also necessary is the integration of technology into all areas of instruction. Various professional organizations may assist in formulating specific knowledge and skill competencies for each of the content areas.

Although the majority of students with learning disabilities have specific difficulty in the area of reading, spelling, or writing (Lyon, 1995), most of these students are placed in general education classrooms. Reading researchers have reached consensus that most reading and spelling disabilities originate with specific impairment of language processing. Therefore, in order to prevent problems in acquiring written language and to provide timely intervention for this major problem, general education teachers (especially in preschool and primary classrooms), special educators, speech-language pathologists, and other school-based personnel must have a thorough knowledge of the structure of oral and written language and its influence on literacy (Moats, 1994). In the content areas for which they are responsible and in other subjects, teachers must demonstrate proficiency in their spoken language, reading, and writing. *Teachers also must be competent to teach word analysis, spelling, reading comprehension, and the writing process.*

Students with learning disabilities also may have problems with mathematical calculations and reasoning. Therefore, general classroom teachers also must have a thorough knowledge and understanding of mathematical concepts and relationships and instructional techniques to assist such students in general education classrooms. Classroom mathematics instruction must be explicit and progress through three levels: concrete, representational, and abstract. Teachers and others who work with students who have learning disabilities need to determine how their students' learning differences affect their acquisition of knowledge. All prospective teachers should be taught how to individualize instruction and how to determine when and how to make accommodations and modifications.

Collaboration among teaching professionals is a relatively new concept. With the current emphasis on mainstreaming (including students with disabilities in general education classrooms), general and special education teachers must work together cooperatively. General educators provide extensive knowledge in content areas; special educators and other specialists bring a variety of instructional techniques and knowledge that are especially beneficial to students with learning disabilities. Too often either the general or the special education teacher is relegated to an ancillary role. *Successful collaboration requires an equal partnership, willingness to collaborate, good communication skills, cooperation among the participating teachers, adequate planning time, and administrative support* (see the paper "Providing Appropriate Education for Students with Learning Disabilities in Regular Education Classrooms," 1990, in this book).

Collaboration may include co-teaching situations in which special educators teach alongside their general education counterparts in the regular classroom. If this is the case, co-teachers may have to learn classroom management techniques and teaching strategies to accommodate their colleagues' teaching styles.

In teacher preparation programs general and special education professors should model collaboration by teaching classes together and designing integrated training programs. Professors involved in successful collaboration should serve as mentors for those entering teaching, those who provide related services, or experienced teachers who embark on new collaborative teaching experiences. Successful practitioners may assist in teaching students the fundamentals of collaborative teaching.

All graduates of teacher preparation programs need the following core competencies to help them work with students who have learning disabilities:

Definitions and Characteristics

- have knowledge of current definitions and characteristics of individuals with learning disabilities and how these disabilities affect students' development and educational performance

Rights and Procedures

- have knowledge of legal rights of the students and parents/guardians and the responsibilities of teachers and schools regarding special education and related services
- have knowledge of procedures for accessing and providing special education and related services (i.e., prereferral, referral, and implementation)

Student Evaluation

- be familiar with commonly used instruments for assessment of students with learning disabilities
- identify informally each child's strengths and weaknesses across developmental areas
- use various formal and informal assessment techniques, including observation, interviews, samples of student work, student self-assessments, and teacher-made tests

- evaluate student performance on an ongoing basis in order to make instructional modifications and referrals when appropriate
- modify/adapt assessment tools in order to meet the specific needs of students with learning disabilities
- use grading procedures appropriate to the needs of students with learning disabilities

Instruction

- develop and implement lesson plans to meet students' unique needs as identified in Individualized Education Programs (IEPs)
- demonstrate knowledge of the continuum of services and placements for students with learning disabilities
- plan and implement instruction in collaboration with the special education teacher when indicated
- modify instruction given students' unique learning characteristics
- modify instruction given such external factors as size of groupings, seating, pace of instruction, and noise level
- adapt technology for students with learning disabilities
- integrate students with learning disabilities into the academic and social classroom community

Social/Emotional Development

- model respect and acceptance of students with learning disabilities
- provide opportunities for meaningful and ongoing social interactions among all students
- recognize and reinforce all student successes, even the small ones, to enhance self-esteem

Classroom Management

- demonstrate various classroom management techniques that assist students with learning disabilities in their social interaction and self-regulation
- facilitate the participation of all students in large- and small-group interaction

Relationships With Families and Colleagues

- promote positive attitudes toward individuals with disabilities and their families
- understand the child's culture and community
- develop an effective partnership with the family in the education of the child
- establish and maintain collegial relationships with school and community

PREPARATION OF SPECIAL EDUCATION TEACHERS

Teachers planning to specialize in learning disabilities must have the core competencies required for general education teachers and an in-depth knowledge of the diverse nature of learning disabilities. A curriculum for preparing learning disabilities teachers should build on the competencies developed in the general education program (see above). To maximize learner outcomes, educators should have an opportunity to apply what they have learned in both supervised classroom settings and through carefully constructed classroom assignments. An earlier paper (see the paper "Learning Disabilities: Issues in the Preparation of Professional Personnel," 1982, in this book) made the point that prospective teachers require ongoing practica and fieldwork to gain comprehensive experience in both general and special education. These practica should be supervised by master teachers and clinicians.

The NJCLD believes that educators who are earning degrees as learning disability specialists should have the following core competencies:

Definitions and Characteristics

- demonstrate an understanding of the major theories, contributors, history, and trends in the field of learning disabilities
- demonstrate an understanding of (a) the characteristics of students with learning disabilities across the developmental spectrum, (b) cultural influences, (c) social/emotional development, and (d) medical interventions

- understand the differences between learning disabilities and other exceptionalities

Rights and Procedures

- know federal, state, and local laws and regulations that directly affect students with learning disabilities
- understand and be able to discuss current legal and ethical issues in special education

Student Evaluation

- evaluate the impact of related factors on a student's learning (e.g., self-regulatory behavior, social perception, social interaction)
- administer and interpret various assessment measures (e.g., formal and informal, achievement- and process-oriented instruments) to identify learning disabilities
- work on a multidisciplinary team to problem-solve and to determine prereferral interventions or eligibility for special education services
- understand the biases and limitations of assessment tools used to identify the abilities and disabilities of diverse learners
- identify and use alternative grading procedures (e.g., oral presentations, projects, portfolios)

Instruction

- demonstrate competence in developing individualized education programs (IEPs) and working with multidisciplinary team to translate diagnostic data into interventions
- determine prereferral intervention strategies for students suspected of having learning disabilities
- match the unique needs of these students with mandated services along the continuum
- demonstrate the ability to use various specialized methods and materials (e.g., multisensory approaches)
- use assistive technology in instruction across the curriculum
- recommend to general educators appropriate academic modifications and accommodations (e.g., extended time on exams,

alternative test formats, spell checkers, audiotaped instructional materials)

- provide instruction in life skills and preparation for transitions from elementary to middle school, middle to high school, and high school to adult living
- provide instruction in learning strategies (e.g., self-monitoring) and organizational strategies (e.g., note-taking, time management, study skills)

Social/Emotional Development

- understand the psychosocial variables affecting self-esteem, behavior, and academic progress
- understand the impact of the complexities and pervasive psychological effects of learning disabilities
- teach students self-awareness (e.g., understanding one's strengths and weaknesses), self-determination (e.g., goal-setting, decision-making and problem-solving), and self-advocacy
- teach students social skills to enhance social competence in school, outside school, and in work settings

Classroom Management

- collaborate with the general education teacher to assist in differentiating between primary behavior problems and those secondary to the learning disability
- develop and implement strategies to help students manage and regulate their behaviors in school

Relationships with Families and Colleagues

- provide effective resource assistance to and/or collaborate with general education teachers
- be involved with various parent and professional organizations and advocate for individuals with disabilities
- be able to collaborate with families to meet the child's special needs in the home
- collaborate and consult with related service providers, administrators, community services agencies, and others in planning for further education, careers, and transition/vocational programming

For more detailed descriptions of competencies of teachers of students with learning disabilities, refer to *What Every Special Educator Must Know: The International Standards for the Preparation and Certification of Special Education Teachers* (1995), Council for Exceptional Children, Reston, VA.

SUMMARY

The NJCLD believes that comprehensive interdisciplinary education programs are necessary for the preparation of all education professionals. To serve the needs of students with learning disabilities most effectively, all preservice teachers should have preparation that includes the competencies described in this paper. Furthermore, professionals who specialize in learning disabilities must have had additional experiences to demonstrate proficiency in all competencies described in this report.

REFERENCES

Council for Exceptional Children. (1995). *What every special educator must know: The International Standards for the Preparation and Certification of Special Education Teachers.* Reston, VA: Author.

Lyon, G. R. (1995). Research initiatives in learning disabilities: Contributions from scientists supported by the National Institute of Child Health and Human Development. *Journal of Child Neurology, 10* (Suppl. 1), 120–126.

Moats, L. C. (1994). The missing foundation in teacher education. Knowledge of the structure of spoken and written language. *Annals of Dyslexia, 44,* 81–104.

Note. The following National Joint Committee on Learning Disabilities papers were cited in this paper, and can be found in this book:

"Providing Appropriate Education for Students with Learning Disabilities in Regular Education Classrooms," 1990

"Learning Disabilities: Issues in the Preparation of Professional Personnel," 1982

Learning Disabilities: Issues in the Preparation of Professional Personnel

A Position Paper of the
National Joint Committee
on Learning Disabilities
September, 1982

THE UNDERSTANDING OF THE NATURE OF LEARNING DISABILITIES AS well as the needs of individuals with these problems has changed within the last 10 years. In response to current issues in learning disabilities, the National Joint Committee on Learning Disabilities has developed previously a series of position papers that address definition (1), inservice programs (2), and educational services (3). This position paper is concerned with the preparation of professional personnel and states problems and recommendations germane to this topic.

The National Joint Committee on Learning Disabilities (NJCLD) believes that there is an urgent need to reevaluate current concepts and practices in the preparation of professionals who will be responsible for the education and management of individuals with learning disabilities. It also is essential that institutions of higher education reevaluate their roles and responsibilities for the preparation of these prospective professional personnel. The NJCLD realizes that professional education* within the professions that deal with learning disabilities will vary according to the specific areas of study required for professional practice. However, the concepts and recommendations included in this position paper are regarded by the NJCLD as appropriate and pertinent to the education of all prospective professionals who will provide service to individuals with learning disabilities.

Any attempt to delineate changes in curricula, including domains of study, curricular sequences, specification of competency standards, and structure of practica, must consider the following problems and issues:

1. Philosophical plurality and the vested interests of some professionals have resulted in diverse differences in professional education.

2. The ability to effect changes in educational policy, curricula and practica has been impeded by the organizational complexity and rigidity of institutions.

3. Competition for diminishing financial resources has fostered separatism and territoriality among professional education programs within institutions of higher education.

4. There is a lack of interdisciplinary (including interdepartmental and intercollegiate) professional education in academic programs and a lack of university incentive to provide for this kind of interdisciplinary education and training.

---

*Professional education refers to coursework, practicum and other educational experiences that take place at the graduate level.

5. The goals of professional education differ from those of accrediting, certifying, or licensing agencies and this difference often has a negative effect on curriculum and training policy.

6. It is increasingly difficult to recruit potentially promising and academically competent personnel into regular and special education at all levels because of salaries that are not competitive, inadequate work environments, and reductions in support services.

7. Many university faculty are distanced from the realities of educational systems and resistant to modifications in professional education programs.

The resolution of these problems and issues will need to occur prior to or simultaneously with bold changes in academic curricula and practica experience.

The NJCLD has developed this position paper based on the belief that the goal of professional education is the development of well-informed and prepared professionals who will meet effectively the educational needs of all individuals. The ability to attain this goal is predicated on the design and implementation of undergraduate, graduate, and professional education programs that will guide and ensure the self-actualization of prospective professionals. After careful consideration of the previously noted problems and a review of current professional education practices in the preparation of professionals who provide services to individuals with learning disabilities and their families, the NJCLD makes the following recommendations regarding professional education.

1. *To meet fully the needs of the learning disabled requires that professionals complete a graduate education program as the minimum level of professional preparation.* Because of the complexities of identifying, assessing, diagnosing and planning of programs for the learning disabled, there is a need to provide personnel preparation at the graduate level to ensure that professionals serving the learning disabled have the knowledge and skills necessary to provide or obtain the comprehensive services that are needed to meet the needs of individuals with learning disabilities.

2. *Institutions of higher education should establish and maintain the highest criteria possible for admission to and continuation of prospective personnel in professional education programs.* Even with the availability of adequate funding, excellent faculty, and appropriate facilities and resources, the quality of the students in a program is the major determinant to the success of that program's efforts to develop well-informed and prepared professionals.

3. *Professional education programs as well as tenured and non-tenured faculty members in institutions of higher education should be evaluated periodically with regard to their respective abilities*

to meet current professional education goals and objectives. It is essential that professional education programs as well as faculty members provide prospective professionals with the knowledge and skills needed to deliver appropriate and effective services to individuals with learning disabilities. This will necessitate evaluation at all levels of the program through such review mechanisms as professional accrediting bodies, state education agencies, peer review, student assessments, or internal administrative review.

4. *Institutions of higher education should design and implement comprehensive guidance, monitoring, evaluation, and support systems in order to ensure accountability in professional education and to allow for individual growth during preprofessional preparation.* Although essential attributes exist that cannot be described adequately within the format of competency statements, much of the knowledge and skill required by professionals is amenable to such a delineation. The advantages of implementing such a competency-based program include (a) increased accountability for programs as a result of requiring students to demonstrate that they have mastered specific competencies the program purports to provide and (b) greater opportunities to systematically individualize a student's program based upon previously acquired skills and knowledge rather than requiring all students to complete virtually identical curricular sequences. Advisors' decision making on a student's course work and practica would be based on the existing and needed competencies of each student, instead of upon transcripts containing generic course titles (e.g., Introduction to Learning Disabilities, Methods of Teaching Learning Disabled Children) that yield little information about the actual skills and knowledge acquired by the student.

5. *Institutions of higher education should establish comprehensive interdisciplinary professional education programs for preparation of professionals.* The need for cooperative interdisciplinary programs in professional education becomes self-evident when consideration is given to the effects of diminishing financial resources for education and training, the extreme variability and lack of uniformity in programs that prepare professionals to provide services for individuals with learning disabilities, the heterogeneous nature of the learning disabilities, and the different manifestations and consequences of the learning disabilities.

The development of cooperative interdisciplinary professional education programs necessitates the following:

a. A review of the roles and responsibilities of institutions of higher education in personnel preparation.

b. The development of cooperative and shared professional education.

c. The establishment of a comprehensive interdisciplinary program that consists of didactic and practica experiences in the following areas:

—Human Development and Its Psychology. This area would include knowledge of human growth, development and its variations, theories of learning, including the basis of motor, cognitive and linguistic development, knowledge of social and emotional growth, and the development of critical thinking and problem solving abilities.

—Theories of Language Acquisition and Use. This area would include knowledge of the interacting components of the language, such as phonology, syntax, semantics and pragmatics; variations in the development of language, discourse and text comprehension; and the relationship of language to school achievement, social and emotional growth.

—Educational Theory and Practice in Learning Disabilities. This area would include knowledge of the nature and manifestations of learning disabilities, including the social and emotional concomitants, the identification and assessment of the individual with learning disabilities, educational/therapeutic management and intervention for the learning disabilities, knowledge and appraisal of teaching/clinical methods, curriculum planning and sequences, systems of teaching content material, systems for the development of adaptive, modified, alternative or unique curriculum, technical support systems, e.g., computer technology, as well as instruction in effective communication with students, their families, other professionals and various publics.

d. The development of clinical consortia professional education centers.

6. *Practica and field experiences in professional education programs must be structured to enable students to demonstrate prespecified competencies in actual teaching/clinical situations.* It is essential that the practica and field experiences provide for comprehensive, graduated, and varied student-centered experiences in regular and special education. These practica and field experiences

must be supervised directly by master teachers and clinicians. The site of the practica or field placement should be selected on the basis of the preprofessional trainees' needs and not simply on the basis of site availability or convenience.

7. *Requirement of a one-year teaching internship should be considered for all students who have otherwise completed a professional education program at an institution of higher education.* Such a prerequisite experience is required currently for professional certification in clinical psychology and speech-language pathology audiology. Although students may acquire the knowledge and skills necessary to implement adequate and appropriate programs for the individual with learning disabilities, their ability to use the knowledge and skills in an actual work experience usually has not been evaluated completely in the program. This evaluation can best take place during an internship year.

The NJCLD is aware of the implications of this recommendation. It will be necessary for state and local education agencies, private school accrediting bodies, institutions of higher education, and professional organizations to work in cooperation to establish guidelines and criteria for the successful completion of the internship year.

8. *Innovative and creative funding patterns and procedures should be explored for the development of model interdisciplinary professional education programs in learning disabilities.* Current funding procedures for professional education programs tend to impede the development of interdisciplinary programs. Institutions of higher education should explore funding methods that will facilitate development of interdisciplinary programs. These would include cooperative efforts among professional organizations, institutions of higher education, private and public foundations as well as local, state and federal agencies.

In order to ensure the design of appropriate and effective professional education programs, institutions of higher education must be responsive to the stated and demonstrated needs of consumers at all levels, including parents, local and state educational agencies, private schools, and most importantly the individual with learning disabilities.

In-service Programs in Learning Disabilities

A Position Paper of the
National Joint Committee
on Learning Disabilities
September, 1981

IN-SERVICE PROGRAMS ARE THE PRINCIPAL MEANS THROUGH WHICH educational agencies change the interaction between teachers and students. It is the position of the National Joint Committee on Learning Disabilities (NJCLD) that systematic in-service programs be established for persons who are responsible for providing programs and services to individuals with learning disabilities. The need for quality in-service programs is motivated by mandates of Public Law 94-142, the lack of consistent pre-service preparation and training in the learning disabilities, and by the recognition that professionals are responsible for the continued enhancement of their competencies. This paper presents some concerns and recommendations of the NJCLD, with regard to the development of in-service programs for professionals who are providing services to individuals with learning disabilities.

In-service programs are most effective when these activities are planned to meet local needs, are equally available to all teachers, administrators and specialists, and when there is clear support and provision made by local boards of education, superintendents, principals, and other administrative officials. However, it is too often the case that deterrents to the provision of effective in-service programs are encountered. Among these deterrents are the following: (a) a lack of appropriate planning and organization of goals and content prior to beginning the program; (b) inappropriate selection and use of personnel in consultative and faculty roles; (c) the presentation of material irrelevant to the needs of the participants; (d) limiting and restricting the scope of participation according to professional roles; and (e) a lack of program availability.

The NJCLD, following a careful consideration of these issues and after reviewing model in-service programs as they currently are used nationally, makes the following recommendations with regard to the design and implementation of in-service programs for professionals who are providing services to individuals with learning disabilities.

1. *The NJCLD recommends that a needs assessment should be conducted prior to the beginning of in-service programs to ensure appropriate planning and implementation of these programs in the area of learning disabilities.*

The design of in-service programs in learning disabilities should be based on an assessment of needs of students and professional personnel, e.g., principals, regular classroom teachers, special educators, learning disabilities specialists, speech-language pathologists and audiologists, reading specialists, school psychologists, vocational educators, and related services staff. When appropriate, the planning and implementation of in-service programs also should include parents and students. Participants should be given an opportunity to establish appropriate objectives and designate the content areas to be included in the in-service program. A prior consideration of needs will establish priorities to meet the participants' goals, define content areas, and result in the use of appropriate consultative services and selection of faculty.

The following content areas, among others, should be considered in the needs assessment and in the planning and implementation of in-service programs.

- Human growth, development and their variations
- The psychology of learning
- The manifestations of learning disabilities
  - spoken language
  - reading
  - written expression
  - mathematics
  - reasoning
- Identification and assessment of the individual with learning disabilities
- Curriculum issues, e.g.,
  - curriculum development, application, and sequence
  - curriculum selection and adaptation of curricular materials
  - alternative curriculum
  - the language of instruction
- Service delivery models in learning disabilities
- Teaching methods in learning disabilities
- Controversial issues in learning disabilities
- Behavioral and other psychological problems in learning disabilities, e.g.,
  - peer relationships
  - social awareness and adjustment
  - drug abuse

— alcohol abuse

— delinquency

- Career and vocational planning for individuals with learning disabilities

- Issues related to the long-term nature of learning disabilities and the necessity for the development of a continuum of educational services (preschool, elementary, secondary, postsecondary)

2. *The NJCLD recommends that the selection of any individual who will provide consultation services or act as faculty for the in-service programs should depend upon the person's competence to address content and to meet the specified goals and objectives of the participants.*

It is essential to evaluate the skills and performance of those who provide consultative services and those who act as faculty. Of primary concern is the ability of consultants and faculty to complete stated objectives in planning and providing in-service programs.

3. *The NJCLD recommends that the models and the content areas of an effective in-service program be based on a comprehensive review of the existing needs of programs, students, and professional personnel.*

Various models for presenting in-service programs should be explored. The models used should be selected following a comprehensive review of existing programs and student needs. It is important that individuals who will participate in the in-service programs have a major role in the planning and design of the in-service model that is used.

Presentation methods should not be restricted to didactic models. Demonstration teaching, the use of case study methods, teleconference arrangements, self-instruction, and the use of teacher assistance teams should not be overlooked. In teacher assistance teams, for example, school-based personnel teams assume primary responsibility for planning and implementing consultative activities within their own school. These individuals should have access to supportive consultative services. The teacher assistance team, in turn, adapts and individualizes the material for local programmatic and professional needs. The National In-service Network* may serve as a resource

---

*Department of Education, Office of Special Education, Washington, DC

for models of effective in-service programs and could be used when design of in-service programs is considered.

Effective in-service programs also must reflect the unique and special needs of various educational settings. The programs should reflect the necessity for continuity of educational planning and ensure the articulation of the curriculum for individuals with learning disabilities. Care must be taken in adapting content to preschool, elementary, secondary, and postsecondary level requirements.

The effectiveness of in-service programs should be evaluated on both the short-term basis (through goal and objective attainment measurements) and on a long-term, longitudinal basis. The only meaningful evaluation in either case will be the changes in performance of individuals with learning disabilities. At the conclusion of the in-service program, on-going school based consultative services should be provided to professional participants so as to facilitate the continued development of newly acquired skills and methods of instruction and treatment.

4. *The NJCLD recommends that multidisciplinary in-service training programs be designed and implemented.*

In-service programs in learning disabilities have been provided by separating personnel according to professional roles. Regrettably, this has prevented appropriate communication among the various professions, e.g., principals, regular classroom teachers, learning disabilities specialists, speech-language pathologists and audiologists, reading specialists, school psychologists, vocational educators, and related services staff. This contradicts the mandate that assessment, planning, and management of individuals with learning disabilities be multidisciplinary in nature.

To meet this mandate, multidisciplinary in-service training models should be developed. This will promote acquisition and use of competencies across the representative professions and increase interprofessional understanding, cooperation, and respect. Separation of personnel according to professional roles for purposes of in-service programs in learning disabilities is not warranted unless the training involves highly specialized skills or knowledge clearly relevant to only one professional group.

5. *The NJCLD recommends that careful consideration be given to issues of availability in the implementation of in-service programs.*

The development and implementation of successful in-service programs must consider availability based on geographic location, physical facilities, and travel time requirements. In-service programs should be designed to meet the needs of personnel in urban, suburban, and rural areas. In addition, cost to participants must be considered and, wherever possible, controlled and minimized.

NOTES

6. *The NJCLD urges all local boards of education, superintendents, principals, and other administrative officials to continue their support of effective in-service programs.*

The NJCLD recognizes the responsibilities of administrative officials to the entire educational system. The NJCLD urges administrative officials, including local boards of education, superintendents, and principals, to advocate for and ensure the viability of in-service programs through (a) personal participation in the programs, (b) development of appropriate and creative incentive programs for participating professionals, e.g., eligibility for credits toward maintenance of certification, tuition credit assistance for college or university coursework, credits toward salary increments, use of extended employment, (c) permitting participation of professionals in the planning, implementation, and evaluation of in-service programs, (d) provision of release time, (e) provision of financial support, and (f) identification of sources for funding in-service programs, e.g., federal, state, local, private, and public sources.

The eventual success of in-service programs ultimately will depend on the clear and consistent support of administrative officials. However, without cooperation at all levels of the educational system these in-service programs will not meet the needs of the students. The goal must always be the development of programs that reflect the needs of education staffs and parents as they work toward meeting the needs of individuals with learning disabilities.

REFERENCE

Education for All Handicapped Children Act of 1975, 20 U.S.C. § 1400 *et seq.*

Preschool and School Issues

A Reaction to *Full Inclusion:* A Reaffirmation of the Right of Students with Learning Disabilities to a Continuum of Services[1]

A Statement of the
National Joint Committee
on Learning Disabilities
January, 1993

---
[1]This statement was developed and approved by representatives of the member organizations only.

THE NATIONAL JOINT COMMITTEE ON LEARNING DISABILITIES (NJCLD) supports many aspects of school reform. However, one aspect of school reform that the NJCLD cannot support is the idea that *all* students with learning disabilities must be served only in regular education classrooms, frequently referred to as *full inclusion*. The Committee believes that *full inclusion,* when defined this way, violates the rights of parents and students with disabilities as mandated by the Individuals with Disabilities Education Act (IDEA).

Because each student with learning disabilities has unique needs, an individualized program must be tailored to meet those needs. For one student, the program may be provided in the regular classroom; yet for another student, the regular classroom may be an inappropriate placement. Therefore, the NJCLD supports the use of a continuum of services and rejects the arbitrary placement of all students in any one setting.

In "Issues in the Delivery of Educational Services to Individuals with Learning Disabilities" (see in this book) the NJCLD stated its support and commitment to "a continuum of education placements, including the regular education classroom that must be available to all students with learning disabilities and must be flexible enough to meet their changing needs." This was reaffirmed in 1991 in "Providing Appropriate Education for Students with Learning Disabilities in Regular Education Classrooms" (see in this book), which recommended that public and private education agencies should "establish system-wide and state-based plans for educating students with learning disabilities in the regular classroom when such placement is appropriate. The responsibility for developing plans must be shared by regular and special educators, parents, and student consumers of the services. Once developed, a plan must be supported at all levels of the educational system."

In summary, the NJCLD supports educational reform and efforts to restructure schools. As stated in "School Reform: Opportunities for Excellence and Equity for Individuals with Learning Disabilities" (see in this book), "NJCLD demonstrates a deep concern and desire that parents, professionals, and policy makers work cooperatively in planning and implementing reforms. We strongly urge that strategies be developed within the reform movement to improve education for students with learning disabilities." As these strategies are developed, it is necessary to ensure that each student with a learning disability is provided a continuum of service options that will guarantee a free, appropriate public education based on the student's individual needs.

REFERENCE

Individuals with Disabilities Education Act of 1990, 20 U.S.C. § 1400 *et seq.*

Providing Appropriate Education for Students with Learning Disabilities in Regular Education Classrooms

A Position Paper of the
National Joint Committee
on Learning Disabilities
June, 1990

MANY CHILDREN AND YOUTH WITH DIVERSE LEARNING NEEDS can and should be educated within the regular education classroom. This setting is appropriate *for some, but not all,* students with learning disabilities. More than 90% of students with learning disabilities are taught in regular education classrooms for some part of their school day (U.S. Department of Education, 1990). When provided appropriate support within this setting, many of these students can achieve academically and develop positive self-esteem and social skills. The regular education classroom is one of many educational program options but is not a substitute for the full continuum necessary to assure the provision of an appropriate education for *all* students with learning disabilities.

In this paper, the National Joint Committee on Learning Disabilities (NJCLD) will identify (a) those factors necessary for an effective educational program for students with learning disabilities, (b) the problems related to serving students with learning disabilities in the regular education classroom, and (c) the recommendations for actions required at the state, school district, and school building level to effectively educate students with learning disabilities within the regular education classroom.

FACTORS RELATED TO EFFECTIVE EDUCATION OF STUDENTS WITH LEARNING DISABILITIES

As early as 1982, the NJCLD took the position that "providing appropriate education for individuals must be the principle concept on which all educational programs and services are developed" (see p. 147 in the paper "Issues in the Delivery of Educational Services to Individuals with Learning Disabilities," 1982, in this book). The NJCLD reaffirms its commitment to and support for the following:

- The education, social, and emotional needs of the individual, the types of disabilities, and the degree of severity should determine the design and delivery of educational programs and services.

- A continuum of education placements, including the regular education classroom, must be available to all students with learning disabilities and must be flexible enough to meet their changing needs.

- Specialized instructional strategies, materials, and appropriate accommodations must be provided as needed.

- Because the educational, social, and emotional needs of students with learning disabilities change over time, systematic and ongoing review of the student's progress and needs is essential to make appropriate adjustments in current educational programs and related services.

- Because learning depends on the quality of the programs and services provided, systematic and ongoing evaluation of programs and their effectiveness in producing desired long-term outcomes is essential.

- Due to the chronic nature of learning disabilities and the changes that occur across the life span of the individual, coordinated educational and vocational planning are required. Therefore, provisions must be made to facilitate transitions that occur at all major junctures in the student's education.

- Social acceptance has a significant impact upon self-esteem of students with learning disabilities. Social acceptance of these students requires the sensitivity of the entire school community.

- To ensure effective mainstreaming of students with learning disabilities, the building principle must set the tone for a positive and accepting learning environment for all children.

PROBLEMS

The NJCLD acknowledges the following problems related to the education of students with learning disabilities in regular education classrooms. Some of these problems are encountered by the teacher in the classroom while others are related to administrative policies and procedures. All of these problems must be addressed by public and private education agencies as plans are developed and implemented for the education of students with learning disabilities.

- The regular education teacher is required to deal with multiple factors including an increasing number of students with diverse cultural and linguistic backgrounds, developmental variations, disabilities, family and social problems, and large class size. The co-occurrence of these factors compounds the situation.

- Many regular education teachers are not prepared to provide the kinds of instruction that benefit a wide diversity of students in the classroom.

- The characteristics of individuals with learning disabilities and the ways in which they interact with curricular demands are not understood by all school personnel.

- Teachers often are required to adhere rigidly to a prescribed curriculum and materials, and, therefore, may not have the flexibility to address the unique needs of students with learning disabilities.

- Adequate support services, materials, and technology often are not available for either the teacher or the student with learning disabilities.

- Time and support for the ongoing planning and assessment that are needed to make adjustments in students' programs and services often are inadequate.

- Schools rarely have a comprehensive plan to evaluate the effectiveness of programs and services for students with learning disabilities, especially those served in regular educational classrooms.

- Coordinated planning is lacking for students with learning disabilities as they make transitions from home to school to work, across levels of schooling and among educational settings.

- Communication concerning students with learning disabilities among administrators, teachers, specialists, parents, and students is often insufficient to facilitate the development and implementation of effective programs.

RECOMMENDATIONS

Implementation of the following recommendations is essential to provide appropriate education for students with learning disabilities in regular education classrooms. Specifically, public and private education agencies should:

- Establish system-wide and school-based plans for educating students with learning disabilities in the regular education classroom when such placement is appropriate. The responsibility for developing plans must be shared by regular and special educators, parents, and student consumers of the services. Once developed, a plan must be supported at all levels of the educational system.

- Establish mechanisms for the development of collaborative relationships among professionals, parents, and students.

- Establish instructional conditions and environments that allow teachers to capitalize on the strengths and remediate or compensate for the weaknesses of students with learning disabilities. These should include:
  - reasonable class size;
  - reasonable paperwork requirements and non-instructional assignments for teachers;
  - appropriate physical environments, including attention to noise levels;
  - sufficient time for teaching and collaborative planning;
  - appropriate materials and technology; and
  - flexibility in determining the array of skills necessary for attainment of overall curricular objectives.

- Ensure the availability of services needed to support the education of students with learning disabilities in the regular education classroom, including:
  - appropriate related services for students;
  - consultation services for teachers;

— direct services for students from teachers certified in the area of learning disabilities and other qualified professionals such as school psychologists, counselors, speech-language pathologists, reading teachers, audiologists, and social workers; and

— teaching assistants/aides trained to work with students who have learning disabilities.

- Provide time and support for planning and communication among and between professionals and parents.

- Ensure the involvement and participation of the regular education classroom teacher in the development and implementation of the Individualized Education Program for students with learning disabilities served in regular education classrooms.

- Establish a system-wide plan for helping students with learning disabilities to make transitions from home to school, from level to level through the school years, and from school to work and life in the community.

- Conduct district and school-building level program evaluation of regular education classroom programs serving students with learning disabilities that focus on student progress and effectiveness of instruction. Based on the evaluation, modifications to the program should be made as needed.

- Require inservice programs for all school personnel to give them the knowledge and skills necessary to provide education for students with learning disabilities in the regular education classroom. The inservice program should be:

— research validated;

— use components other than the single workshop format; and

— include activities to help participants learn strategies to meet individual needs of students, foster attitudes conducive to educating students with learning disabilities in the regular education classroom, and promote collaboration.

- Provide inservice programs for those school personnel who have not previously had such training in the following areas:

- child and adolescent development
- individual differences
- spoken and written language development and disorders
- cognitive development and learning theory
- social and emotional development
- cultural diversity
- nature of learning disabilities
- informal assessment
- validated instructional strategies
- adaptation of instructional materials and teaching techniques
- classroom management
- collaboration, consultation, and team teaching
- multidisciplinary team interaction
- parent and family support

The NJCLD acknowledges that implementation of these recommendations is challenging. For schools to succeed in educating students with learning disabilities in the regular education classroom, there must be a careful analysis of the factors which contribute to effective education and attention to the problems and recommendations included in this paper. A plan of action must be developed and implemented.

REFERENCE

U.S. Department of Education. (1990). *To assure the free appropriate public education of all handicapped children: Twelfth annual report to Congress on the implementation of the Education of the Handicapped Act.* Washington, DC: U.S. Department of Education, Office of Special Education and Rehabilitative Services.

Note. The following National Joint Committee on Learning Disabilities paper was cited in this paper, and can be found in this book:

"Issues in the Delivery of Educational Services to Individuals with Learning Disabilities," 1982

Learning Disabilities and the Preschool Child

**A Position Paper of the National Joint Committee on Learning Disabilities
February, 1985**

THE NATIONAL JOINT COMMITTEE ON LEARNING DISABILITIES (NJCLD) is concerned about the early identification, assessment, planning, and intervention for those preschool children who demonstrate specific developmental delays or deficit patterns that often are early manifestations of learning disabilities.[1] These manifestations include atypical patterns of development in cognition, communication, motor abilities, and/or social and personal behaviors that adversely affect later academic learning. Development in each of these areas is characterized by individual differences as well as variability in rates and patterns of maturation.

It is during the preschool years that developmental disorders of different types and degree are first suspected or recognized. Because the preschool years represent a critical period during which essential prevention and intervention efforts are most effective, professionals and families must attend to the needs of preschool children whose development is characterized by patterns of specific deficits.

Learning disabilities is a term that refers to a heterogeneous group of disorders[2] (see the paper "Learning Disabilities: Issues on Definition," 1981, in this book) of presumed neurological origin manifested differently and to varying degrees during the life span of an individual (see the paper "Adults with Learning Disabilities: A Call to Action,": 1985, in this book). These disorders or manifestations of such disorders are developmental in nature and must be viewed as problems not only of the school years, but also of preschool years, and continuing into adult life. During the preschool years, learning disabilities frequently are manifested as specific deficits in language and speech development, reasoning abilities, and other behaviors requisite to early academic achievement. These deficits may occur concomitantly with problems in self-regulation, social interaction, or motor performance. Various manifestations of learning disabilities may be seen in the same child at different ages and as a result of learning demands. This perspective is especially important to maintain when dealing with the preschool child.

Normal development is characterized by broad ranges of individual and group differences, as well as by variability in rates and patterns of maturation. During the preschool years, this variability is

---

[1] As used in this paper, the word *preschool* includes the period from birth through kindergarten age.

[2] As defined by the NJCLD, learning disabilities is a generic term that refers to a heterogeneous group of disorders manifested by significant difficulties in the acquisition and use of listening, speaking, reading, writing, reasoning, or mathematical abilities. These disorders are intrinsic to the individual and presumed to be due to central nervous system dysfunction. Even though a learning disability may occur concomitantly with other handicapping conditions (e.g., sensory impairment, mental retardation, social and emotional disturbance) or environmental influences (e.g., cultural differences, insufficient/inappropriate instruction, psychogenic factors), it is not the direct result of those conditions or influences.

marked. For some children marked discrepancies in abilities are temporary and are resolved during the course of development and within the context of experiential interaction. For other children, there is a persistence of marked discrepancies within and among one or more domains of function, necessitating the child's referral for systematic assessment and appropriate intervention.

ISSUES IN EARLY IDENTIFICATION[3]

The purpose of identification programs is to find children who are suspected of having handicapping conditions. In preschool children the identification program includes the examination of at-risk indicators,[4] systematic observation of the child, and the use of screening tests and other procedures. All early identification programs should be based on procedures that are reliable and valid. Once children are identified they will require comprehensive assessment and systematic follow-up services.

An effective identification program must take into account the numerous biological and environmental factors that influence the course of a child's development during the preschool years. Procedures used for initial identification or screening are not a substitute for comprehensive assessment. Furthermore, identification programs that are not followed by assessment, intervention, and follow-up services are futile.

At-Risk Indicators

Professionals often use indicators that are acknowledged to be associated with adverse developmental outcomes as a basis for determining that a child is at-risk for learning disabilities. The use of at-risk indicators should be only one step in determining the status and needs of the child and serves as an initial basis for referral and continued monitoring of a child's growth and development.

---

[3] As used in this paper *identification* refers to any and all initial steps taken to select children who are suspected of having handicapping conditions.

[4] As used in this paper, *at-risk indicators* refer to biological, genetic, and perinatal events as well as adventitious diseases or trauma that are known to be associated with adverse developmental outcomes.

At-risk indicators do not always predict which child is in jeopardy of future developmental deficits or which aspects of development will be delayed or disordered. Caution should be used when informing parents about the presence of these indicators. For example, some children with a history of perinatal complications may develop normally, while other children without such histories may demonstrate specific patterns of deficits that will require careful assessment and intervention. Children whose histories suggest that they are at-risk for learning disabilities should be observed carefully by means of frequent and periodic examination in order to ascertain whether growth and development follow expected patterns.

Systematic Observations

Reliance on at-risk indicators is not a substitute for systematic observations of the child's behaviors and abilities. These observations should provide a description of the presenting concerns as well as information regarding the frequency, persistence, and severity of the behaviors causing concerns. When a question is raised about the integrity of development, the family should be so advised, and the child should be referred to qualified professionals or to a preschool assessment team for clarification of these observations. This is an essential activity if effective planning and implementation of appropriate treatment is to occur.

Screening Tests and Other Procedures

A third approach to early identification is the use of screening instruments and procedures, such as testing, teacher rating scales, and locally constructed measures. Careful consideration of reliability, validity, and standardization of the screening instruments and procedures is essential in their selection, use, and interpretation. Although the predictive validity of total scores for certain screening tests has been established, the use of individual items to predict later developmental status or plan remedial programs cannot be justified. Screening tests and other procedures are not to be used for diagnosis, planning, placement, or treatment. All children who have been identified as a result of screening and who are suspected of having a specific learning disability should be referred to professionals appropriately qualified in the deficit areas for assessment, evaluation, and follow-up services.

Assessment of Children During the Preschool Years

Referral of the child for assessment of developmental status depends on data and information collected during the screening process. When a specific developmental problem is suspected, the family and the child should be referred to appropriately qualified professionals who will conduct an integrated assessment of cognition, communication, motor abilities, sensory functions, and social-emotional development. Determination of the child's status and needs depends on a comprehensive assessment of the child's functioning in the following domains:

1. sensory functions, including haptic, auditory, and visual systems;

2. motor functions, including gross and fine motor abilities;

3. cognition, including perceptual organization, concept formation, and problem solving;

4. communication, including language comprehension, production, and use; and

5. behavior, including temperament, attention, self-regulation, and social interaction patterns.

An interdisciplinary approach must be used in obtaining and interpreting assessment information that is derived from a wide variety of sources, including direct observations of the child. The specific patterns of abilities and disabilities must be determined.

In some cases, an extended period of assessment and observations will be necessary to determine a child's status and needs. Time-limited placement in a diagnostic preschool setting can be a useful means for addressing diagnostic questions, determining the child's developmental age, abilities, and deficits, and evaluating various methods of intervention for the individual child. Responsible professionals should ensure the orderly transfer of the child to the appropriate setting as soon as a decision concerning the child's status and needs has been reached. Such a process reduces the risk that children will be indiscriminately or prematurely labeled as learning disabled.

The child's developmental age and accomplishments as well as previous opportunities and experiences will determine the extent to which early academic skills are present on entering school. The variability seen in a child's readiness for academic learning and instruction reflects cognitive, communicative, social, and emotional growth as well as physical and neurological maturation. Readiness for academic instruction is more related to differential rates of development than to chronological age. An integrated perspective on the child's functioning in various areas of growth and development is essential. This perspective must be maintained when interpreting assessment results and planning educational placement and instructional approaches that are appropriate to the child's status and needs.

Delivery of Preschool Services

Selection of the appropriate program and specific intervention strategies for the preschool child with specific patterns of deficits is predicated on the clear understanding of how these deficits influence overall learning and development. Program selection and the choice of intervention strategies must be determined following a comprehensive and integrated interdisciplinary assessment.

Decisions pertinent to program selection and placement are influenced by many factors. Among these factors are the following:

- the types of disabilities and the degree of severity;
- the philosophy of the service provider or agency;
- the professional preparation, experience, and attitudes of service personnel;
- the kinds of intervention strategies and resources available within public or private preschool programs;
- the ability of the family to facilitate the child's development in the home environment; and
- geographic constraints.

Various agencies and professionals are responsible for services to the child during the preschool years. Consequently, cooperation among those agencies and professionals who plan and implement preschool education and intervention programs is critical. As the child is moved from one service setting to another, coordination and orderly transfer of information among agencies and professionals are essential to ensure continuity of services.

Preschool programs for the child with specific deficits must provide periodic review of the child's status, including a review of the placement, curriculum, and intervention approaches. Only careful monitoring of the child's progress can lead to a determination of the effectiveness of the child's program.

No single approach to intervention can be expected to serve as a panacea for the different needs presented by preschool children with specific deficits. Alternative and modified methods of intervention must be available. Appropriate consultative and direct services by professionals from different disciplines should be used as necessary.

The primary focus of intervention should be on activities appropriate for the child's developmental age and directly related to the enhancement of functioning in the area(s) of the child's disability. Traditional readiness activities in preschool programs often are not sufficient to ensure later school success. Early intervention programs should focus on ameliorating the deficits that affect the current functioning of the child as well as facilitate the development of abilities, skills, and knowledge considered to be requisites for later academic, linguistic, and social functioning.

A continuum of program and service options must be available if preschool children with specific developmental deficits are to be served appropriately. Programs should be mandated through appropriate federal and state legislation. State agencies need to enforce a continuum of service options, provide appropriate funding, and promote interagency cooperation between the public and private sectors.

THE FAMILY

In some cases, parents are the first to suspect their child may have a problem and should address their concerns by consulting with qualified professionals. In other cases, some families initially may deny the existence of a problem because they are fearful of or threatened by its possibilities and consequences. Because family acceptance and cooperation are both critical to effective intervention, differences in family responses must be recognized and appropriate support services provided.

The family serves as an important source of information about the child's status and needs. Similarly, it is essential that the family understand and help to implement the programmatic goals established for their child. Family members should have access to a range of support services, including the following:

- assistance in recognizing, understanding, and accepting the child's problems;

- assistance in developing effective ways to manage and facilitate the child's development in the home environment;

- assistance in program selection; and

- assistance in locating parent support networks and programs.

Direct family involvement in the preschool program is a major factor in effectiveness. The family has responsibility for the application and generalization of learned skills and adaptive behaviors into the home environment and will consequently require open communication with professionals who provide services to the child. They also need to be included in the development of program policy and advocacy efforts.

ISSUES IN PERSONNEL PREPARATION

Qualified personnel are necessary to meet the needs of preschool children, especially those with developmental deficits. Competency standards for personnel providing these preschool services are required. Professional education programs must provide an understanding of the principles of normal child development and disorders in the domains of cognition, communication, motor development, sensory function, social-emotional adjustment, and academic development (see the papers "In-service Programs in Learning Disabilities," 1983; and "Learning Disabilities: Issues in the Preparation of Professional Personnel," 1985; in this book.)

Physicians, nurse practitioners, allied health professionals, and other related service providers should receive systematic preparation in the identification and referral of preschool children with suspected deficits. These individuals should be knowledgeable about the range of programs and services available to the child and family. Similarly, education personnel and day-care providers should receive systematic instruction about normal development, indicators of learning disabilities and other developmental disorders, methods of screening, and procedures for referral. In this way, assessment and appropriate intervention can be initiated as early as possible. Similarly, all individuals concerned with services for the preschool child must develop appropriate strategies to achieve effective interaction with the child's family.

NEEDS AND RECOMMENDATIONS

To meet the needs of the preschool child with developmental deficits, the NJCLD recommends the following:

1. Systematic identification programs for all preschool children should be instituted.

    a. Individuals who work directly with preschool children must learn to identify those children with suspected deficits and must know how, as well as to whom, these children should be referred for assessment.

    b. Procedures for developmental review and early identification of disabilities must be validated, developed, and implemented on a cost-effective basis.

    c. Technically adequate instruments for screening of preschool children must be developed.

2. Assessment procedures should be based on an interdisciplinary approach that explores all possible sources of the child's present problems and provides an integrative statement of the child's status and needs.

    This requires that:

    a. professional preparation programs provide multiple theoretical bases for understanding the contributions of various factors to children's development as well as to their problems; and that

    b. professionals from various disciplines work in collaboration to ensure that comprehensive evaluations are provided as necessary.

3. Early intervention programs should be available to all preschool children with identified developmental deficits.

   a. Federal and state agencies must mandate, fund, and monitor the development and implementation of preschool diagnostic and intervention programs for children with patterns of specific deficits for the ages 0-6 years.

   b. There must be validation of public and private service delivery models in urban, suburban, or rural areas that are appropriate to the needs of children with various developmental deficits.

4. Personnel qualified in the deficit area are necessary to meet the needs of preschool children who demonstrate patterns of specific deficits.

   a. Professional preparation programs for personnel who will work with preschool children with developmental deficits should include instruction in normal child development as well as its disorders.

   b. Preschool teachers, early childhood specialists, and daycare providers must be knowledgeable about identification and appropriate referral of preschool children suspected of developmental delays or deficits.

   c. Preschool and daycare programs must be staffed by qualified personnel who have learned to use a variety of intervention strategies appropriate to the needs of the children enrolled within these settings.

5. Families should be assisted in participating fully in all phases of identification and treatment of a preschool child with specific patterns of deficits. In order to accomplish this, certain needs must be met.

   a. Parental participation must be encouraged and welcomed.

b. Parents must be provided with support services that will enable their full and active participation.

c. Efforts must be made to develop parent education materials and programs that explain the child's needs and detail the intervention strategies to be implemented by the family.

6. Professionals should provide information to the public concerning issues about child development and its disorders.

    a. Guidelines should be developed that will provide the public with information about the roles and responsibilities of various professionals in the identification, assessment, and treatment of children with developmental disorders.

    b. Professionals should develop and use networks that will facilitate referrals of children and their families to appropriate service providers and agencies.

7. All professionals and agencies responsible for the identification, assessment, and treatment of children with developmental disorders must recognize and respond to the unique requirements necessary to meet the needs of the non-English or limited English speaking population.

    a. Individuals involved in the identification, assessment, and treatment of non-English or limited English speaking preschool children must ensure that neither language barriers nor cultural differences will influence findings and recommendations.

    b. Programs that provide services to non-English or limited English speaking preschool children with developmental disorders must have available qualified personnel who can provide appropriate services to these children.

    c. Assessment instruments and instructional materials should be developed to ensure adequate assessment and treatment of non-English speaking or limited English speaking children with developmental disorders.

    d. Information about child development and its disorders must be developed for use with non-English speaking or limited English speaking families to enhance their understanding of their children and their special needs when present.

8. Systematic research must continue to address issues related to identification and provision of services for preschool children with developmental deficits.

   a. What refinements are necessary in the use of at-risk indicators in order to maximize their prognostic value?

   b. What indices of early behavior best predict or correlate with later personal and social adjustment?

   c. What indices of early behavior predict or correlate with later academic learning?

   d. What factors contribute to the success of various intervention programs and strategies?

REFERENCE

Note. The following National Joint Committee on Learning Disabilities papers were cited in or consulted for this paper, and can be found in this book:

"Learning Disabilities: Issues on Definition," 1982

"In-service Programs in Learning Disabilities," 1983

"Adults with Learning Disabilities: A Call to Action," 1985

"Learning Disabilities: Issues in the Preparation of Professional Personnel," 1985

Issues in the Delivery of Services to Individuals with Learning Disabilities

A Position Paper of the
National Joint Committee
on Learning Disabilities
February, 1982

PROVIDING APPROPRIATE EDUCATION FOR INDIVIDUALS MUST BE the principal concept on which all educational programs and services are developed. The right of an individual to an appropriate education must be ensured. For children, youth, and adults with learning disabilities to receive appropriate education, alternative and modified instruction is necessary as well as a diverse range of services provided by professionals with differing preparation, skills, and expertise. It is the position of the National Joint Committee on Learning Disabilities (NJCLD) that special education programs and support services for individuals with learning disabilities must be part of an education agency's total instructional program and must not be regarded as a separate and parallel system. Provision of appropriate education requires that a continuum of public and private educational programs and services and a variety of instructional strategies be available for all individuals from early childhood throughout life.

There are challenges that must be addressed in developing a continuum of educational programs and services. One challenge is related to financial constraints that may influence establishment of program priorities. Nevertheless, it remains the responsibility of education agencies to provide a continuum of appropriate educational programs and services for individuals with learning disabilities. This can be achieved by the application of creative management strategies as well as judicious and innovative use of resources.

The NJCLD has developed this position paper based on the principle that the goal of education is to prepare each individual to function effectively and productively as a self-sufficient and contributing member of society. After a careful consideration of issues pertinent to service delivery and after reviewing model service delivery programs, the NJCLD makes the following recommendations with regard to services for individuals with learning disabilities.

1. *The planning, design, and implementation of appropriate service options and instructional strategies are predicated upon all concerned professionals having a clear understanding of what learning disabilities are* (see the paper "Learning Disabilities: Issues on Definition," 1981, in this book), *and the manner in which these different disabilities modify how an individual learns.* The selection of instructional strategies or the type of educational placement must be determined by a comprehensive and integrated assessment derived from multidisciplinary evaluation(s) of the individual at risk for learning disabilities. Multidisciplinary decision-making rather than

token participation by various personnel is essential for the delivery of effective services.

Decisions pertaining to placement and programming within the public and private sector are influenced by the following: the individual's learning characteristics; the educational philosophy of the agency; the competence, experience, and attitudes of professional personnel within the public and private sector; geographic constraints; and the instructional strategies and resources inherent within each educational placement. Once selected, the educational placement and instructional strategies must be reviewed periodically and systematically. This review should effect appropriate program modifications based on a recognition of changes in the individual's needs. Throughout their lives, individuals with learning disabilities may be at risk for unnecessary failure. Consequently, a review system must be provided throughout an individual's school career to ensure that appropriate educational services are provided when needed.

2. *The types of disabilities and the degrees of severity determine the characteristics of the service options.* The NJCLD recommends the development of the following types of service options for individuals with learning disabilities. Within the continuum of service options presented below, it is implicit that comprehensive assessments, monitoring of the individual's progress, systematic observation, review of curriculum, instructional approaches, and placement as well as careful follow-up will be included. Appropriate consultative services by professionals from different disciplines should be available and used effectively. Flexibility of scheduling, improved interprofessional communication, and coordination of services are essential.

SERVICE OPTIONS

I. This option is a regular education program placement in which the teacher receives consultative assistance from appropriate professionals. It is essential that the teacher be provided with assessment procedures as well as instructional approaches through demonstration teaching.

II. This option is for individuals who are able to function primarily in a regular education program with specialist consultation provided to the teacher, but who also require direct service assistance from specialized personnel. These services can be provided either in the regular educational program (e.g., individual tutoring, small group instruction) or in a separate setting (e.g., resource room, clinical setting). In Option II placement, the number of service providers dealing with the individual may increase.

III. This option is for individuals who require primary placement in a specialized education program while participating in selected aspects of the regular education program. The extent of integration will be a function of the individual's abilities in relation to program options. The direct provision of services by specialized personnel to the individual or teacher must be available and used as needed.

IV. This option is for individuals who require placement in a specialized education program at a non-residential facility, e.g., self-contained classroom or special school. The direct provision of services by specialized personnel to the individual or teacher must be available and used as needed.

V. This option is for individuals who require placement in a specialized education program at a residential facility. Generally, this placement is for individuals whose learning disabilities are accompanied by other disorders or for those for whom an appropriate specialized educational program is not available at a non-residential facility.

Although other options exist for the education of individuals with learning disabilities, it is not within the scope of this paper to provide a complete review of these models. However, it is important to state that some placements, e.g., multi-cross categorical programs, are not always appropriate for individuals with learning disabilities unless these programs provide for instruction by personnel with knowledge of learning disabilities, provide for comprehensive assessment and planning, and maintain the use of alternative or modified methods of instruction that will meet the unique learning needs of individuals with learning disabilities. Regardless of the service option, provision must be made for careful integration of all information related to the diagnosis and education of the individual with learning disabilities.

3. *The long-term nature of learning disabilities necessitates a continuity of programs and services.* The full range of programs and services should be designed and implemented for individuals with learning disabilities at all age levels, preschool through post-secondary. Aspects of the service delivery change over time. For instance, the needs of children from age 3 to 9 years are markedly variable. The use of diagnostic teaching with this age group is necessary and may need to be continued from the preschool years through the primary grades. When properly applied, the information gained from diagnostic teaching can avoid the danger of assigning a child to a particular type of service that might otherwise be inappropriate.

At the other end of the continuum, individuals with learning disabilities at the secondary level should have access to a variety of alternative services. Such alternatives might include the following: career/vocational planning, counseling, and education; the use of vocational rehabilitation services; tutoring in the academic content areas; compensatory approaches to learning; basic skills education; teaching learning and life-skills strategies, and counseling and preparation for college attendance.

4. *For individuals with learning disabilities, the primary instructional or remedial focus should be on activities directly related to the enhancement of functioning in the areas of manifested disabilities, i.e., listening, speaking, reading, writing, reasoning, and mathematics.* While the primary educational intervention should focus on the academic, linguistic, and cognitive natures of the disabilities, effective intervention also must, when necessary, address such correlates as hyperactivity, disorders of attention, learning styles, and issues of self-image and control, as well as problems in social relationships. These may all exacerbate the existing disabilities.

5. *Professional personnel who provide services to individuals with learning disabilities must possess the flexibility to offer a variety of instructional approaches.* Rigid adherence to partisan pedagogical perspectives about assessment and intervention is indefensible because of the diversity of existing individual needs and the wide variety of strategies, technology, and resources available to meet the needs of individuals with learning disabilities.

6. *Parents of and individuals with learning disabilities should be given maximal opportunities for a meaningful involvement in the educational programs.* Regardless of the competence of professional personnel in providing services, programs for individuals with learning disabilities will be limited to the extent that the special commitment and abilities of both parents and affected individuals are not used. Therefore, opportunity must be provided to parents of and individuals with learning disabilities to participate actively in the educational process.

7. *Educational administrators, including program directors, principals, and curriculum specialists, should assume an active and formal role in advocating for the interests of individuals within the educational setting.* Administrators as well as all professional personnel and faculties must become more knowledgeable about the theoretical and practical issues involved in providing optimal services for individuals with learning disabilities. This can be achieved through the provision of in-service programs which are the principal means through which the educational agencies change the inter-

NOTES

action between teachers and students (see the paper "In-service Programs in Learning Disabilities," 1981, in this book). In addition, educational administrators must accept the primacy of their role in holding the individual as the focus of all planning. For example, time should be provided for teachers and specialized personnel to plan and discuss the needs of the individual with learning disabilities so that effective education may occur. The focus in the education of individuals with learning disabilities must be instruction. This can be achieved only through the cooperation of parents, students, educational administrators, teachers, and specialized personnel in the planning and implementation of appropriate curriculum, instructional approaches, and service options.

Note. The following National Joint Committee on Learning Disabilities papers were cited in this paper, and can be found in this book:

"Learning Disabilities: Issues on Definition," 1981

"In-service Programs in Learning Disabilities," 1981

Transition, Postsecondary, and Adult Issues

Learning Disabilities: Issues in Higher Education

A Position Paper of the
National Joint Committee
on Learning Disabilities
January 29, 1999

COLLEGE AND UNIVERSITY PRESIDENTS UNDERSTAND THE BENEfits of educating a diverse student body. Students with learning disabilities represent a significant segment of this group. This paper addresses emerging issues relative to students with learning disabilities on college and university campuses. The intended audience for this paper includes college and university presidents, administrators, faculty, and professional support staff.

Because of the wide variance in postsecondary institutions in such terms as size and mission, there is little consistency in the way that institutions provide services to students with learning disabilities. As students with learning disabilities pursue not only undergraduate education but graduate and professional education as well (Henderson, 1995), it is becoming increasingly critical for institutions to review both their mission and philosophies as they work toward an integrated model of service provision.

Section 504 of the Rehabilitation Act of 1973 and the Americans with Disabilities Act (ADA) have articulated the rights of individuals with learning disabilities in higher education. The laws mandate that postsecondary institutions provide equal access to programs and services for students with learning disabilities. Given their interpretation of such legislation, individual colleges and universities are at various stages in the development and integration of policies and procedures for providing accommodations to students with disabilities.

Previous papers from the National Joint Committee on Learning Disabilities (NJCLD) have addressed learning disabilities across the life span (see the paper "Learning Disabilities: Issues on Definition," 1990, in this book) and transition services for students with learning disabilities (see the paper "Secondary to Postsecondary Education Transition Planning for Students with Learning Disabilities," 1994, in this book). These papers serve as a prelude to this paper, which focuses on programming for undergraduate students enrolled in 2- and 4-year colleges and universities, graduate students, and students in professional schools. This paper articulates the impact of college and university missions and their policies and procedures on students with learning disabilities. The paper concludes with recommendations for creating a responsive campus environment.

COLLEGE AND UNIVERSITY STUDENTS WITH LEARNING DISABILITIES

The NJCLD defines learning disabilities as "... a heterogeneous group of disorders manifested by significant difficulties in the acquisition and use of speaking, reading, writing, reasoning, or mathematical abilities. These disorders are intrinsic to the individual, presumed to be due to central nervous system dysfunction, and may occur across the life span...." (see p. 23 of the paper "Learning Disabilities: Issues on Definition," 1990, in this book).

Successful individuals with learning disabilities tend to be goal-oriented, determined, persistent, and creative (Reiff, Gerber, & Ginsberg, 1993). Persons with these characteristics are often an asset to the university community. Many students with learning disabilities are aware of their disabilities before matriculation. Some students, such as nontraditional and returning students, are not diagnosed with learning disabilities until after their admission to college. Once diagnosed, it is the student's responsibility to disclose his/her learning disability and the extent to which it affects academic access (Lynch & Gussel, 1996). A student's eligibility for services, and the particular type of service he/she needs, must be based on appropriate documentation (Brackett & McPhearson, 1996, Larson & Aase, 1997). With appropriate accommodations it is more likely that students with learning disabilities will experience a successful college career. Witte, Philips, and Kakala (1998) in their study at a major university found that students with learning disabilities were competitive academically with their peers and graduated with grade point averages not significantly below the control group. This study also found that students with learning disabilities on average took only one semester longer to graduate.

INSTITUTIONAL MISSION

Presently, institutions are establishing learner outcomes for all programs. While students with learning disabilities should be expected to meet the institution's academic standards, they should be given the opportunity to fulfill learner outcomes in alternative ways. The process by which students with learning disabilities demonstrate mastery of academic standards may vary from that of the larger student body, but the outcomes can and should remain the same. Accommodating students with learning disabilities need not jeopardize the academic standards of the institution.

While the Americans with Disabilities Act and Section 504 of the Rehabilitation Act require institutions to make academic adjustments to provide equal access, they do not require postsecondary institutions to make changes to essential elements of the curricula and therefore do not compromise curricular standards (Scott, 1994). The courts and the Office of Civil Rights (OCR) have been clear that postsecondary institutions can and should establish policies that identify and maintain those essential components of the college curriculum [*Guckenberger, et al. v. Trustees of Boston University, et al.*, 974 F. Supp. 106 (D.Ma, 1997); *Rancho Santiago Community College* (CA), 3 NDLR 52 (OCR, Region IX, 1992); *Bennett College* (NC) OCR Case No. 04-95-2065 (Region IV, 1995)]. A team approach to reviewing the institution's mission and its policies for evaluating its essential programmatic elements results in a balanced and integrated plan for both academic integrity and educational access. Faculty and staff from the various programs can work to outline essential program components in relation to the institution's mission. Collaboration among administrators, faculty members, and disability service professionals should ensure that academic standards are delineated and maintained.

Although the team approach to policy design may involve a number of administrative offices, it is highly recommended that services for students with disabilities, including those for students with learning disabilities, be housed within the administrative structure that promotes a strong academic focus and shared faculty responsibility for providing accommodations. For some campuses that office reports directly to the president or provost; for others, disability issues may be under the purview of the academic or student affairs offices.

POLICY ISSUES

It is essential to have written policies that ensure that students with learning disabilities receive the same high-quality education as their peers. These policies should address the issues of admission, documentation of a learning disability, accommodations, and curriculum modifications. It is important that students be made aware of the existence of an appeal process which is set forth in writing. Students should have easy access to all written policies and procedures including the appeal process. Such documents should be available in a variety of formats, in all appropriate campus literature, and through available technology, such as a Web site, which all students can access.

Admission Policy

Colleges and universities vary in their admission requirements and policies; some have open admissions, while others have rigid entry requirements. Most students with learning disabilities meet the standard admission criteria and will not be readily identifiable during the admission process. However, some students with learning disabilities may appeal the standard entry requirements because of the effects of their disability on their academic performance or test scores. Within the appeal process for admission, available to all students, a mechanism is needed to consider the impact of a student's learning disability on his/her academic record. During the appeal process, it is important to recognize that inconsistencies in the student's academic record may reflect the presence of his/her learning disability. It is recommended that the admission appeal process for students with learning disabilities involve a team approach to decision making. It is imperative that the team consist of institutional representatives who are knowledgeable about learning disabilities.

Documentation Policy

As noted in the NJCLD definition, learning disabilities occur throughout the life span. Whether a college or university accepts a student's documentation as adequate or requires additional information before providing services, accommodation decisions should be addressed on an individual basis. The campus learning disability professional, in conjunction with the student, should evaluate the effects of the student's disability in relation to the curriculum and academic standards. During this process, faculty and other campus representatives may be consulted to review the academic environment and its relationship to the student.

Appropriate Accommodations

A learning disability is not static; its effects may change in relation to a number of student, environmental, and curricular factors. Such factors as the student's abilities, the classroom setting, methods of instruction, or task demand may entail the need to provide differing academic adjustments. These accommodations, to be requested by the student, must be made on a case-by-case basis to ensure the integrity of the academic program and the educational experience. Requests for accommodations must be responded to in a timely fashion. The decision-making process for academic adjustments may involve the faculty member, the student, and the learning disabilities professional. Identifying and selecting appropriate accommodations require an analysis of the task, the student's disability, course objectives, and faculty input. Examples of accommodations may include but are not limited to the following: alternative test formats, extended time, alternative access to oral and written material, and course substitutions (Journal of Learning Disabilities, 1996).

There are a number of new technologies and software options available that foster access to academic materials, such as text-to-speech, speech synthesizers, visual outliners, reading programs, textbooks on tape, print enlargers, visual tracking, phonetic spell checkers, and other emerging technologies. It is critical that technology on campus be reviewed and made accessible to students with disabilities (R. Riley, personal communication, September 7, 1997).

Curriculum Adjustments

The federal laws and subsequent court decisions make it clear that colleges are not expected to make changes in the curriculum that compromise essential components of a program. In certain well-documented cases, a student may be unable to meet all of the requirements of a degree program. For example, a student seeking a bachelor's degree in nursing must complete all required courses in the program. However, if such a student had a history of poor performance in the acquisition of a second language that was directly linked to a learning disability, that student might then petition for substitution of a different requirement in place of the foreign language requirement.

Before course substitutions are considered, an evaluation of the course's purposes and outcomes should be conducted. Alternatives to course substitutions might include alternative testing, alternative evaluation of performance, and course audits. Because both the integrity of the academic program and the educational experience of the student are at stake, policy of this magnitude should be established and implemented through shared decision making. A team including the faculty member, disability service provider, student, and a learning disability specialist constitutes a balanced forum for decision making.

Acceptable course substitutions to be considered by college personnel include the following: culturally oriented courses, anthropology courses, or sign language in place of foreign language courses; logic, philosophy, or computer science courses as an alternative for a math requirement. The team making this decision should consider the individual's disability in relation to the student's chosen academic program (Tucker, 1996). It should be noted that proportionately very few students with learning disabilities petition for course substitutions (Sparks, Philips, & Ganschow, 1996).

RECOMMENDATIONS FOR CREATING A RESPONSIVE CAMPUS ENVIRONMENT

In recent years many questions have emerged during the development of services for students with learning disabilities: What documentation is necessary to determine eligibility for which services? What are the institution's responsibilities to modify a curriculum? What constitutes true access to education? Kroeger and Schuck (1993) give specific directives for creating a responsive environment. The authors call for organizing and structuring services, further defining access to higher education, clarifying of available sources and allocations of funding for services, and consistently evaluating services and the model for collaborating with faculty. Following are recommendations for building a responsive campus community to provide appropriate services to students with learning disabilities.

A. Review the Structure of the Institution
- Ensure that written college and university policy statements regarding services for students with learning disabilities are consistent with the mission of the institution
- Review all campus literature for statements of equal access and the procedures students with learning disabilities must follow to request services
- Consider housing the office for disability services in academic affairs or a similar administrative office for effective reporting and support

B. Establish Policies
- Ensure confidentiality of student information
- Develop written policies and procedures, including the appeal processes, regarding students with learning disabilities in the areas of admission, documentation, academic accommodations and curriculum adjustments

- Make policies and procedures available to the entire campus community via student handbooks, catalogs, and course schedules in alternative formats

C. Promote Awareness
- Establish mechanisms for dissemination of information about learning disabilities to students, administration, faculty, and service professionals
- Disseminate information to the campus community about available services
- Familiarize faculty, staff, administration, and students with laws governing accommodations for students with learning disabilities
- Clearly designate the individuals who make the decisions regarding accommodations so that intrafaculty or staff disputes are minimized

D. Collaborate
- Build campus expertise through collaboration and consultation
- Establish a team of service providers and faculty members for decision making in regard to admission, documentation, academic adjustments and program accommodations for students with learning disabilities
- Remain current regarding disability issues
- Provide cost effective, reasonable accommodations for students with learning disabilities

CONCLUSION

The purpose of this paper is to provide recommendations related to institutional mission, policies, and accommodations for students with learning disabilities in higher education. Building an academic community responsive to diverse student populations, including students with learning disabilities, benefits the college community as well as society. Students with learning disabilities have individual strengths, weaknesses, and academic needs—as do all students. While it is important to consider individually the status of students with learning disabilities, it is critical that academic institutions plan for the admission and consequent education of these students. When colleges and universities examine their mission, develop policy, and work together as a campus community, education of individuals with learning disabilities can be greatly enhanced. Policies should address the issues of admissions, documentation of a learning disability, accommodations, and curriculum modifications.

Ensuring the education of students with learning disabilities is a campus-wide responsibility. Bringing the campus community together for shared decision making requires campus-wide awareness of students with learning disabilities, an understanding of the legal requirements for access, a review of essential program components, and a structuring of service delivery that is compatible with the school's mission. This institutional commitment and planning will allow students, faculty, and administration to work together toward their common goal: successful higher education for students with learning disabilities.

REFERENCES

Americans with Disabilities Act (ADA), 42 U.S.C. § 12101 *et seq.*

Bennett College (NC) OCR Case No. 04-95-2065 (Region IV, 1995).

Brackett, J., & McPhearson, A. (1996). Learning disabilities diagnosis in postsecondary students: A comparison of discrepancy-based diagnosis models. In N. Gregg, C. Hoy, & A. Gay (Eds.), *Adults with learning disabilities: Theoretical and practical perspectives* (pp. 68–84). New York: Guilford Press.

Guckenberger, et al., v. Trustees of Boston University, et al., 974 F. Supp. 106 (D. MA, 1997).

Henderson, C. (1995). *College freshmen with disabilities: A statistical profile.* Washington, DC: HEATH Resource Center.

Journal of Learning Disabilities. (1996). *29*(4).

Kroeger, S. & Schuck, J. (1993, Winter). Moving ahead: Issues, recommendations, and conclusions. In *New directions for student services* (pp. 103–110). San Francisco: Josey-Bass.

Larson, N., & Aase, S. (1997). *From screening to accommodation: Providing services to adults with learning disabilities.* Columbus, OH: AHEAD.

Lynch, R. T., & Gussel, L. (1996, March/April). Disclosure and self-advocacy regarding disability-related needs: Strategies to maximize integration in postsecondary education. *Journal of Counseling and Development, 74,* 352–357.

Rancho Santiago Community College (CA), 3 NDLR 52 (OCR, Region IX, 1992).

Rehabilitation Act of 1973, 29 U.S.C. § 701 *et seq.*

Reiff, H. B., Gerber, P. J., & Ginsberg, R. (1993). Definitions of learning disabilities from adults with learning disabilities: The insiders' perspectives. *Learning Disability Quarterly, 16,* 114–125.

Scott, S. (1994). Determining reasonable academic adjustments for college students with learning disabilities. *Journal of Learning Disabilities, 27,* 403–412.

Sparks, R., Philips, L., & Ganschow, L. (1996). Students classified as learning disabled and the college foreign language requirement. In J. Liskin-Gasparro (Ed.), *Patterns and policies: The changing demographics of foreign language instruction* (pp. 123–159). Boston: Heinle & Heinle.

Tucker, P. B. (1996). Application of the American with Disabilities Act (ADA) on Section 504 to colleges and universities: An overview and discussion of special issues relating to students. *Journal of College and University Law, 23(1),* 1–4.

Witte, R., Philips, L., & Kakala, M. (1998). Job satisfaction of college graduates with learning disabilities. *Journal of Learning Disabilities, 31,* 259–265.

Note. The following NJCLD papers were cited in this paper, and can be found in this book:

"Learning Disabilities: Issues on Definition," 1990

"Secondary to Postsecondary Education Transition Planning for Students with Learning Disabilities," 1994

Secondary to Postsecondary Education Transition Planning for Students with Learning Disabilities

A Position Paper of the
National Joint Committee
on Learning Disabilities
January, 1994

THE NATIONAL JOINT COMMITTEE ON LEARNING DISABILITIES (NJCLD) is concerned that many students with learning disabilities do not consider postsecondary education options (two- and four-year colleges and vocational schools) because they are not encouraged, assisted, or prepared to do so. The NJCLD believes that many students with learning disabilities should select postsecondary education options and that they can succeed in their pursuit of them if transition plans are designed and implemented effectively.

Providing transition plans and services is crucial when assisting youth with disabilities to prepare for adult life. Comprehensive transition planning needs to address several domains, including education, employment, personal responsibility, relationships, home and family, leisure pursuits, community involvement, and physical and emotional health. In this report, the NJCLD will address the rationale for the transition planning process as it applies to the education of students with learning disabilities, specifically the progression from secondary to postsecondary education. The roles and responsibilities of those involved also will be outlined.

RATIONALE

Transition planning is mandated in the Individuals with Disabilities Education Act (IDEA), formerly the Education for All Handicapped Children Act (PL 94-142). The transition planning requirements in IDEA, which include development of an individualized transition plan, ensures that planning is initiated in middle school and continued through high school. Transition planning and services focus on a coordinated set of student-centered activities designed to facilitate the student's movement from school to post-school activities, including postsecondary education. Transition planning for students with learning disabilities must remain flexible and reflect the developmental and educational needs of the students at different grades and times. It also must reflect a clear understanding of the learning disability, as well as the specific abilities and needs of the student. Planning should link the student's transition goals to effective and efficient services.

ROLES AND RESPONSIBILITIES

Transition planning is a student-centered activity that requires a collaborative effort. Responsibilities are shared by the student, parents, secondary personnel, and postsecondary personnel, all of whom are members of the transition team.

Student Roles and Responsibilities

The students' participation, along with support from other team members, is central to transition planning and decision making. This includes asking the student to identify preferences and interests and to attend meetings on transition planning. Success in postsecondary educational settings depends on the student's level of motivation, independence, self-direction, self-advocacy, and academic abilities developed in high school. Student involvement in transition activities must be initiated *as early as possible* and no later than age 16.

To contribute to successful transition planning, the student should

- understand his or her specific learning disability, including its effect on learning and work;

- establish realistic goals;

- present a positive self-image by stressing strengths, while understanding the influence of the learning disability;

- know how, when, and where to discuss and request needed accommodations;

- develop personal qualities, such as realistic self-assessment, willingness to take risks, and ability to sustain efforts;

- develop and use social skills;

- develop and apply effective studying, test-preparation, test-taking, time-management, and note-taking strategies;

- seek instructors and learning environments that are supportive;

- maintain an ongoing personal file that includes school and medical records, individualized education program (IEP), resume, and samples of academic work;

NOTES

- know rights and responsibilities necessary to prepare for and to access postsecondary education;
- identify and access resources that will provide needed support;
- explore postsecondary education options and entrance requirements;
- select courses that meet postsecondary requirements; and
- prepare for and participate actively in the postsecondary application process.

Parent Roles and Responsibilities

The primary role of parents during transition planning is to encourage and support students to plan and achieve their educational goals. Parents also should encourage students to develop independent decision-making and self-advocacy skills.

To contribute to successful transition planning, parents should

- be involved in transition planning and ensure that the student is also included;
- help the student develop realistic goals;
- encourage the student to develop future educational plans and to explore realistic postsecondary options;
- help the student select high school courses that meet postsecondary requirements;
- collaborate with secondary and postsecondary staff to make decisions regarding programs, services, and resources;
- help the student collect and maintain an ongoing personal file that includes school and medical records, IEP, resume, and samples of academic work;
- communicate confidence in the student's ability to be successful in a postsecondary setting; and
- encourage the student to develop maximum independence in the learning, study, and living skills critical to success in postsecondary settings

Secondary School Personnel Responsibilities

Secondary school personnel and administrators, through their own involvement, must show students how to look beyond high school toward postsecondary education. This is accomplished by initiating, designing, and evaluating effective transition plans and coordinating services that are consistent with federal and state statutes, rules, and regulations. An essential role is that of the transition team coordinator, who guides and monitors the implementation of individual student transition plans.

To contribute to successful transition, secondary school personnel should

- form a transition team consisting of a coordinator, the student, the parent(s), administrators, teachers, and related service personnel;

- include the student and parents in the entire planning process;

- demonstrate sensitivity to the culture and values of the student and family;

- develop an appropriate packet of materials to document the student's secondary school program and to facilitate service delivery in the postsecondary setting;

- provide administrative support, resources, and time to foster collaboration among team members;

- inform the student about statutes, rules, and regulations that ensure his or her rights;

- provide appropriate course selection, counseling, and academic support services;

- ensure competency in literacy and mathematics;

- ensure that the student learns effective studying, time-management, test-preparation and test-taking strategies;

- help the student use a range of academic accommodations and technological aids, such as electronic date books, videodisc technology, texts on tape, grammar and spell checkers, and word processing programs;

- help the student to evaluate his or her dependence on external supports and adjust the level of assistance when appropriate;

- help the student develop appropriate social skills and interpersonal communication abilities;

- help the student to develop self-advocacy skills, including a realistic understanding of the learning disability and how to use this information for self-understanding and communication with others;

- foster independence through increased responsibility and opportunity for self-management;

- encourage the student to develop extra-curricular interests and to participate in community activities;

- promote the student's self-esteem and self-confidence;

- encourage the student to develop extra-curricular interests and to participate in community activities;

- inform the student and parent(s) about admission requirements and demands of diverse postsecondary settings;

- inform the student and parent(s) about services that postsecondary settings provide, such as disabilities services, academic services, and computer-based writing services;

- ensure the timely development of documentation and materials in keeping with application time lines;

- help the student and parent(s) select and apply to postsecondary institutions that will offer both the competitive curriculum and the necessary level of learning disability support services; and

- develop ongoing communication with postsecondary personnel.

Postsecondary Personnel Responsibilities

Postsecondary personnel must network with, and disseminate information to, secondary educators, parents, and prospective students to realistically frame the expectations for the rigors of the postsecondary experience. Providers of services for students with learning disabilities in postsecondary education settings must be prepared to meet the needs of a diverse student population who have a variety of skills, educational backgrounds, and intellectual abilities.

To contribute to successful transition planning, postsecondary personnel should:

- provide linkages to high schools through outreach efforts;
- inform secondary school personnel of the prerequisites for the transition to postsecondary options;
- disseminate information about college/vocational school preparation and the expectations associated with various postsecondary settings;
- offer "LD college nights" at local high schools and at state conferences;
- provide opportunities for campus visits for prospective students and their families, educating them about the unique features of the specific postsecondary program;
- help students to effectively negotiate postsecondary settings;
- offer summer orientation programs on the admissions application process, admissions requirements, and general postsecondary education program survival skills;
- clarify the roles of the student and the service provider in a postsecondary setting;
- offer comprehensive orientation programs to students with learning disabilities who have elected to attend a given institution;
- teach students how to advocate for themselves in the postsecondary setting;
- advocate on behalf of students, when necessary, to ensure that their rights are safeguarded under Section 504 and the Americans with Disabilities Act (ADA);
- negotiate "reasonable academic adjustments" with faculty and administration that will maintain the integrity of the curriculum;

- establish written policies and procedures concerning admissions, diagnosis, accommodation, curriculum requirements, and service delivery to students with learning disabilities;

- work closely with admissions officers to ensure that students with learning disabilities are fairly considered;

- act as a liaison to the greater college/vocational school community, and inform them about serving students with learning disabilities; and

- provide faculty and staff development on learning disabilities.

SUMMARY

For many students with learning disabilities, participation in postsecondary education is appropriate. However, to achieve this goal, comprehensive transition planning is essential. The primary objective of this planning is to help the student select, access, and succeed in a postsecondary education program.

This planning involves contributions from four groups: the student, parent(s), and secondary and postsecondary education professionals. The result of effective transition from a secondary to a postsecondary education program is a student with a learning disability who is confident, independent, self-directed, and in actual pursuit of career goals. A student with a learning disability can succeed in the transition from secondary to postsecondary education settings if the student, parents, and professional personnel work together to design and implement effective transition plans.

REFERENCES

Education for All Handicapped Children Act of 1975, 20 U.S.C. § 1400 *et seq.*

Individuals with Disabilities Education Act of 1990, 20 U.S.C. § 1400 *et seq.*

Rehabilitation Act of 1973, 29 U.S.C. § 701 *et seq.*

Adults with Learning Disabilities: A Call to Action

**A Position Paper of the National Joint Committee on Learning Disabilities
February, 1985**

LEARNING DISABILITIES ARE A HETEROGENEOUS GROUP OF DISorders of presumed neurological origin that persist into adult life to varying degrees and with different outcomes. Although many adults with learning disabilities are successful, many are not. A large number of adolescents with learning disabilities do not complete high school. Still other individuals have difficulty gaining admission to or completing postsecondary education programs including college or vocational preparation courses.

The National Joint Committee on Learning Disabilities (NJCLD) is concerned with those issues related to learning disabilities as manifested in adults. The purpose of this position paper is to identify these issues and to propose ways for exploring and resolving the problems encountered by adults with learning disabilities.

The following concerns need to be addressed when the problems of adults with learning disabilities are considered.

1. Learning disabilities are both persistent and pervasive throughout an individual's life. The manifestations of the learning disability can be expected to change throughout the life span of the individual.

2. At present there is a paucity of appropriate diagnostic procedures for assessing and determining the status and needs of adults with learning disabilities. This situation has resulted in the misuse and misinterpretation of tests that have been designed for and standardized on younger people.

3. Older adolescents and adults with learning disabilities frequently are denied access to appropriate academic instruction, prevocational preparation, and career counseling necessary for the development of adult abilities and skills.

4. Few professionals have been prepared adequately to work with adults who demonstrate learning disabilities.

5. Employers frequently do not have the awareness, knowledge of, nor sensitivity to the needs of adults with learning disabilities. Corporate as well as public and private agencies have been unaware and therefore have failed to accept their responsibility to develop and implement programs for adults with learning disabilities.

6. Adults with learning disabilities may experience personal, social, and emotional difficulties that may affect their adaptation to life tasks. These difficulties may be an integral aspect of the learning disability or may have resulted from past experiences with others who were unable or unwilling to accept, understand, or cope with the persons' disabilities.

7. Advocacy efforts on behalf of adults with learning disabilities currently are inadequate.

8. Federal, state, and private funding agencies concerned with learning disabilities have not supported program development initiatives for adults with learning disabilities.

In light of these concerns, the NJCLD makes the following recommendations.

1. *Programs must be initiated to increase public and professional awareness and understanding of the manifestations and needs of adults with learning disabilities.* A coalition is needed among professionals, adults with learning disabilities, and parent groups that will design and provide systematic programs to inform the public about adults with learning disabilities. The program should include information about the following:

- the heterogeneity of learning disabilities;

- the characteristics as well as the persistent and pervasive nature of learning disabilities;

- the changing manifestations of learning disabilities;

- the variations in cognition, communication, and individual learning styles demonstrated by adults with learning disabilities;

- the social and emotional consequences of learning disabilities for adult adjustment; and

- the implications of learning disabilities for future academic or career achievements.

An understanding of these facts is essential for effective planning, design, and implementation of appropriate education and vocational training programs.

2. *Selection of appropriate education and vocational training programs and employment for adults with learning disabilities is predicated on a clear understanding of how their condition influences their learning and performance.* Program selection and the choice of intervention strategies must be based on the results of a comprehensive and integrated assessment of the individual that will provide a description of specific patterns of abilities and disabilities.

Decisions pertinent to program selection and placement are influenced by many factors. Among these factors are the following:

- the individual's patterns of abilities and disabilities;

- the skills required for successful performance in a specific work setting;

- the available range of instructional or training program options;

- the availability of community and on-job support services (e.g., counseling, support groups), as well as consultative and direct therapy services;

- the education and vocational training philosophy of the service or employment agency;

- the competence and experience of those professionals and other individuals providing services for adults with learning disabilities; and

- the attitudes and beliefs of those within the public and private sector about adults with learning disabilities.

3. *Throughout the school years, individuals with learning disabilities must have access to a range of program and service options that will prepare them to make the transition from secondary to postsecondary or vocational training settings.* Continued emphasis on remediation of basic academic skills, provision of adaptive curricula, and enhancement of study skills is important. It is also imperative to provide programs that will facilitate the development of social and interpersonal skills as well as employable skills. This may require radical changes in some of our current practices.

- Continuing review is necessary throughout the school years so as to monitor the individual's current status and needs. This review of the individual's status and needs is essential if responsible professionals are to ensure that appropriate education and prevocational services are provided.

- Career counseling and vocational programs should be initiated during the early school years. Adults with learning disabilities and their parents should be provided with information concerning ranges of career options and programs. Selection of career options must be based on an appreciation of their abilities.

- To facilitate social adaptation, counseling as well as individual and peer group experiences should be provided for students with learning disabilities. These experiences are intended

    —to enhance interpersonal and social skills;

—to foster an ability to deal with new situations;

—to develop an appreciation for oneself; and

—to foster the development of autonomy, self-advocacy, and independent living skills.

4. *Alternative programs and services must be provided for adults with learning disabilities who have failed to obtain a high school diploma.* Many adults with learning disabilities fail to achieve a high school diploma. Some adults with learning disabilities are school dropouts, while others remained in school but were unable to meet minimum competency test requirements necessary for the high school diploma. Few of these individuals ever pursue the General Equivalency Diploma or other alternatives to achieve the diploma. In response to these observations, the following actions are recommended:

- Educate school personnel about those factors that are predictive of school dropout.

- Mandate federal, state, and local authorities to establish programs for truancy and school dropout prevention for individuals with learning disabilities.

- Educate individuals with learning disabilities about alternatives available to them in achieving the high school diploma.

5. *Adults with learning disabilities must have an active role in determining the course of their postsecondary or vocational efforts.* To facilitate that role, all concerned with assisting adults who have learning disabilities need to ensure their

- right to choose and opportunity to decide,
- knowledge of options and responsibilities of choice,
- right to risk and invest in their choice,
- opportunity to learn through experience and failure,
- right to change employment settings and activities.

6. *Consistent with the Rehabilitation Act of 1973 and regulations implementing Section 504 of that Act, appropriate federal, state, and local agencies as well as postsecondary and vocational training programs should continue the development and implemen-*

tation of effective programs that will allow adults with learning disabilities the opportunity to attain career goals. Also, consistent with Section 504, postsecondary programs, colleges, vocational schools, employers, and governmental agencies should be aware of the nondiscriminatory testing requirements for the handicapped. If adults with learning disabilities are to gain access to and profit from postsecondary or vocational training programs, innovative planning and collaborations will be necessary among those agencies and personnel working with and concerned for their needs. These planning consortia should include adults with learning disabilities and also may include their families.

a. Postsecondary Programs—Those persons responsible for planning postsecondary programs for individuals with learning disabilities should establish an interdisciplinary advisory council that will develop, implement, and monitor necessary procedures and services. Such procedures and services should include, among others, the following:

- admission criteria and procedures;
- assessment procedures for determining the individual's status and needs;
- guidelines for course selection and sequences;
- guidelines on alternative methods for evaluating the student's learning of course content material (e.g., oral instead of written examinations and the use of untimed examinations);
- support systems that will assist, as needed, with the development of study skills, reasoning abilities, and decision-making skills as well as the enhancement of listening, speaking, reading, writing, and mathematical abilities;
- the use of modified methods of instruction as indicated;
- the opportunity for individual and group psychological assistance;
- the establishment of peer support groups; and
- the opportunity for career counseling.

b. Vocational Training—The Rehabilitation Act of 1973, including Section 504, mandates that vocational training programs be available to adults with learning disabilities. In response to the law, public and private sectors have developed diverse and often unrelated programs for vocational training and preparation. The consequent lack of interagency planning and program coordination has caused confusion. This has prevented many adults with learning disabilities from gaining access to appropriate training programs. If responsible vocational training agencies and rehabilitation centers are to meet successfully the needs of adults with learning disabilities, these agencies and centers should coordinate plans and guidelines that will address among other issues the following:

- referral procedures;
- eligibility criteria;
- assessment procedures and methods;
- counseling procedures and program planning;
- job placement, job holding, employment retention, and follow-up procedures;
- employment performance and evaluation procedures; and
- procedures for provision of support services as needed.

c. Employment Opportunities—Education and rehabilitation agencies should develop effective liaisons with business, industry, unions, and civil service employment agencies. These networks are essential to facilitate the transition, training, and employment of adults with learning disabilities. In addition, these liaisons and networks will ensure appropriate management of adults currently in the workforce. Finally, the armed forces should design and implement effective programs for the assessment's training and care of adults with learning disabilities who are within the various service branches.

Employers should develop an awareness and knowledge of the needs of adults with learning disabilities. Having identified the skills required to complete a specific job, industry will need to collaborate with vocational rehabilitation and training agencies in preparing adults with learning disabilities to enter and successfully remain within the workforce. Many adults with learning disabilities will need to use vocational, technical, and continuing adult education programs, and other community resources to acquire skills and abilities necessary to compete actively and succeed in the workforce.

7. *The development of systematic programs of research that will address the status and needs of adults with learning disabilities is*

essential for the provision of appropriate services. Among the many issues that need to be addressed are the following:

- the types, characteristics, and changing manifestations of learning disabilities during the course of adult growth;

- the relationship between learning disabilities and adult psychosocial maladjustments, including substance abuse, depression, and suicides;

- the performance differences of adults with learning disabilities in various educational, mental health, and vocational settings;

- the status and needs of adults with learning disabilities who are in prisons;

- the patterns of outcomes for adults with learning disabilities who dropped out of or graduated from public or private secondary education programs;

- the impact of minimum competency testing requirements for individuals with learning disabilities; and

- the effects of minimum competency test modifications on the pass and fail rates among individuals with learning disabilities.

8. *Curricula must be developed and incorporated in preparation programs for professionals in such disciplines as education, vocational and rehabilitative counseling, social work, psychology, medicine, and law to inform these professionals about the problems and needs of adults with learning disabilities.* While preparation of personnel who provide services to individuals with learning disabilities is presented elsewhere (see the paper "Learning Disabilities: Issues in the Preparation of Professional Personnel," 1982, in this book), it is important to emphasize continuing education as a principal means for providing professionals currently in practice with information about the problems and needs of adults with learning disabilities.

9. *Mental health professionals must be aware of the unique personal, social and emotional difficulties that individuals with learning disabilities may experience throughout their lives.* For some individuals, these difficulties may be an integral aspect of the learn-

ing disability. For many others, these emotional difficulties result from life experiences. The emotional difficulties are manifested in different forms that include, among others, disturbed patterns of interaction with spouses and children and disturbances in social relations. Throughout their lives some individuals with learning disabilities have interacted with teachers, parents, peers, and others who were not prepared or willing to understand their needs or to help them cope with their problems. These nonfacilitating interactions contributed to the development of severe emotional disorders for some individuals.

Mental health professionals must be prepared to prevent and treat the possible psychological sequelae associated with persistent learning disabilities. These sequelae might include, but not be limited to, antisocial behavior, chronic depression, suicide, and substance abuse. For adults with learning disabilities, the inevitable consequences of attempts to cope in a society that makes demands without understanding and that imposes without sensitivity are all too apparent.

REFERENCE

Rehabilitation Act of 1973, 29 U.S.C. § 701 *et seq.*

Note. The following National Joint Committee paper was cited in this paper, and can be found in this book:

"Learning Disabilities: Issues in the Preparation of Professional Personnel," 1982

Policy Issues

Learning Disabilities and the Americans with Disabilities Act (ADA)

A Position Paper of the
National Joint Committee
on Learning Disabilities
September, 1992

ON JULY 26, 1990, THE AMERICANS WITH DISABILITIES ACT (ADA) was signed into law. The ADA is a civil rights law that prohibits discrimination against persons with disabilities. It was designed to remove barriers that prevent individuals with disabilities from enjoying the same opportunities that are available to persons without disabilities.

The ADA requires that persons with disabilities, including those with learning disabilities, have access to and be accommodated in employment, transportation, public accommodations, state and local government activities, and communication. The following information will assist entities covered by the ADA to achieve voluntary compliance with the requirements of ADA as related to individuals with learning disabilities.

How Does the ADA Relate to Learning Disabilities?

- The ADA defines disability as "a physical or mental impairment that substantially limits one or more of the major life activities of an individual." The ADA lists specific learning disabilities as one possible physical or mental impairment, and learning is included as a major life activity.

What Is a Specific Learning Disability?

- Individuals with learning disabilities may have difficulty in one or more of the following: listening, speaking, reading, writing, spelling, and mathematics. They also may have problems in reasoning, remembering, organizing, managing time, and social skills.

- Learning is a lifelong process that continues beyond the school years. Learning disabilities affect how people learn throughout their lives.

- Specific learning disabilities are not the same as learning problems that result from mental retardation, blindness, deafness, or emotional disturbance.

- Individuals with learning disabilities also may have extraordinary talents and learning capabilities. For example, a person who reads poorly may be a great mechanic or computer wizard.

WHAT ARE THE EFFECTS OF LEARNING DISABILITIES?

- The effects of learning disabilities vary with the individual, setting, and stage of life. Not all individuals with learning disabilities are affected in the same way or to the same degree.

- The difficulty a person with learning disabilities may experience will vary with:
  - Type and severity of disability
  - Ability to compensate for the disability
  - Familiarity with the task
  - Complexity of the task
  - Work, training, or school setting
  - Access to assistive devices, support, and services
  - Degree of support from others

HOW ARE INDIVIDUALS IDENTIFIED AS HAVING LEARNING DISABILITIES?

- Learning disabilities may be identified at any point during an individual's life span. During the school years, diagnostic teams may identify learning disabilities.

- A significant number of persons may not have been identified as having learning disabilities during their school years. However, it may be determined that they

NOTES

in fact are limited in one or more major life activities by learning disabilities. Therefore, they are eligible for programs and services under the ADA.

POTENTIAL BARRIERS FOR INDIVIDUALS WITH LEARNING DISABILITIES

- Physical/environmental barriers
  - Inappropriately designed instruction manuals or testing material
  - Long or complex directions
  - Noisy or visually distracting work settings
- Attitudinal/behavioral barriers
  - Impatient or inflexible teachers, job supervisors, or peers
  - Lack of understanding that individuals with learning disabilities have many capabilities

WHAT CAN BE DONE TO MINIMIZE BARRIERS?

- Ways to minimize physical/environmental barriers:
  - Provide auxiliary aids and use assistive technology (spelling devices, electronic calculators)
  - Reduce visual or auditory distractions
  - Change activity site (quieter, less distractions)
  - Provide international symbols, illustrations, or other signage modifications
  - Provide memory aids or cue cards

- Ways to minimize attitudinal/behavioral barriers:
  - Encourage appropriate attitudes and behaviors of managers and peers
  - Use peer coaches or mentors to provide guidance
  - Ask students or employees what works best for them
  - Encourage individuals to ask questions
  - Recognize and use the individual's abilities

WHAT ARE POSSIBLE TASK ACCOMMODATIONS AND MODIFICATIONS?

- Analyze the job and develop effective accommodations
- Supplement training and instruction using alternative materials and methods (visual, auditory, manipulative)
- Simplify information
- Clearly spell out expectations
- Organize tasks into meaningful steps
- Demonstrate by example, and provide practice
- Provide both written and spoken instructions
- Allow additional time to complete tasks
- Modify ways to complete tasks
- Modify techniques for evaluating task performance

WHAT POLICIES AND PRACTICES NEED TO BE MODIFIED?

- Policies that discriminate when reasonable accommodations and modifications would enable appropriate performance of persons with learning disabilities.

- In employment settings, discriminatory policies and practices include:
  - Time-limited examinations
  - Policies for certification or licensing examinations that do not allow for alternative ways to complete the examination
  - Employment based solely on one criterion, such as a written test or oral interview
  - Not allowing job restructuring
  - Hiring, evaluation, promotion, grievance, termination practices that are discriminatory
- In educational settings, discriminatory policies and practices include:
  - Admission and placement procedures that are discriminatory
  - Policies that do not allow for flexibility in use of curriculum and instruction
  - Discriminatory evaluation practices
  - Promotion/retention policies that do not accommodate individuals with learning disabilities
  - School completion/graduation requirements that discriminate against individuals with disabilities

What Is the Best Way To Ensure Cost-Effective ADA Compliance?

- Obtain technical assistance and consultation from experts in the area of learning disabilities.
- Match job skills with employee abilities.
- Evaluate the facility and services for accessibility.
- Develop a plan to remove barriers and to improve accessibility.

- Modify discriminatory policies, practices, and procedures.
- Determine and obtain auxiliary aids and services needed by individuals with learning disabilities.

THE BOTTOM LINE

- Ask people with learning disabilities about their needs.
- Show respect and sensitivity for people with disabilities.
- Use what works.
- Use your resources creatively and effectively.

This document provides general information to promote voluntary compliance with the Americans with Disabilities Act (ADA). It was developed by the National Joint Committee on Learning Disabilities (NJCLD). Any opinions or interpretations in the document are those of the National Joint Committee on Learning Disabilities. The Americans with Disabilities Act and associated regulations should be consulted for further, more specific guidance.

REFERENCE

Americans with Disabilities Act of 1990, 42 U.S.C. § 12101 *et seq.*

School Reform: Opportunities for Excellence and Equity for Individuals with Learning Disabilities— A Special Report[1]

**A Statement of the National Joint Committee on Learning Disabilities
June, 1991**

---

[1]This statement was developed and approved by representatives of the member organizations only.

NOTES

THE NEWLY ARTICULATED GOALS FOR EDUCATION IN THE UNITED States, many of which are set forth in *America 2000: An Education Strategy,* cannot be achieved without important school reform. The National Joint Committee on Learning Disabilities (NJCLD) joins with others in calling for school reform and for the development of strategies to improve education. The NJCLD urges that the needs of students at risk for school failure, including those with learning disabilities, be addressed when setting new goals, policies, and practices. This is essential if schools are to meet the diverse learning needs of these students, optimize their achievement, and ensure effective educational outcomes. To ignore the abilities and potentially rich contributions of students with learning disabilities will create imbalance and inequity within the educational system, restrict the quality of life for individuals, and diminish the nation's competitive status within a global economy.

The NJCLD cautions that professionals and parents must be aware of the goals of school reform and restructuring if they are to participate in the development of new initiatives that achieve a balance between excellence and equity. The intent of this special report is to stimulate thought and discussion about reform initiatives and positive action on behalf of individuals with learning disabilities. The purposes of this report are

1. to identify important components of the reform movement and explore their implications for individuals with learning disabilities, and

2. to encourage active participation by professionals and parents in the reform process by suggesting questions that must be addressed if the needs of all students are to be met.

The NJCLD has identified eight components that must be considered when addressing issues of school reform and developing strategies to improve education: (a) academic standards and student achievement, (b) curriculum and instruction, (c) accountability and evaluation, (d) school and classroom organization, (e) locus of decision making, (f) choice, (g) school finance, and (h) personnel preparation.

Academic Standards and Student Achievement

Higher academic standards and more demanding and uniform expectations for student performance are major goals of the reform movement. Program initiatives include increased graduation requirements, national testing programs, additional course work and homework, strict adherence to grade retention policies, and the use of differential diplomas.

Although higher academic expectations is a worthy goal for America's students, more demanding and uniform standards will pose several problems for students with learning disabilities and those responsible for their education. First, because a large number of students will fail to meet the higher academic requirements, there will likely be an inordinate increase in the number of students identified as having learning disabilities. Second, as schools and school personnel are judged largely on the ability of their students to meet uniform standards, the development of a variety of curricular options and instructional strategies may be less likely. Third, the large percentage of students with learning disabilities who are unable to meet higher academic standards will be at risk for dropping out of school. Finally, for those students with learning disabilities who remain in school, the development of rigid standards will keep many from becoming eligible for postsecondary programs and give them fewer opportunities as adults.

Questions to Consider

- What educational options are available to students who do not or cannot meet uniform standards?

- Are there policies that allow school personnel to adjust standards on behalf of students with learning disabilities in an equitable way?

- What policies and procedures exist to encourage and assist students who do not meet uniform standards to stay in school?

- To what extent are teachers prepared and permitted to modify learning goals and design individual instructional approaches that will meet the needs of students with learning disabilities?

- Are homework policies and assignments appropriate for individual students?

- How do schools and families address students' needs to become responsible for their own learning and develop other skills not commonly measured by tests of school achievement?

- Do schools have a reasonable policy for promotion and retention of students, and are decisions about promotion or retention based on thoughtful consideration of the individual student's needs?

- What are the criteria for granting diplomas to students with learning disabilities who have difficulty meeting uniform standards?

- Do school personnel make realistic recommendations that facilitate transition to postsecondary schooling or employment?

CURRICULUM AND INSTRUCTION

School reform movements often focus on restructuring curriculum and instruction, particularly by establishing uniformity. Given this focus a danger exists that curricular options vital to the successful achievement of students with learning disabilities may not be available to them. This is especially true as uniform standards are established and implemented. The desire to include all students within regular education should not overshadow the fact that some students with learning disabilities need to learn different content in different ways. When standards focus on learning discrete facts, the goals and types of instruction available for students with learning disabilities are limited. For example, exclusive focus on scholastic achievement will not meet the needs of students with learning disabilities who must be taught to function independently, or be prepared for direct entrance into the work force. As academic standards are increased, there will likely be a concurrent increase in the development of new instructional and service delivery models. It is vital that these new models incorporate instructional approaches and service delivery systems that have been researched and validated with students who have learning disabilities. Such approaches and systems include both effective teaching practices and appropriate support services.

Questions to Consider

- Do the planning, design, and implementation of curricular programs and instructional strategies reflect an understanding of what learning disabilities are and how such disabilities affect the way individuals learn?

- Are different curricular options and instructional strategies available to serve individuals with different types of learning disabilities and degrees of severity?

- Are curricular continuity and transition planning a part of educational programs?

- Does the curriculum include content related to the acquisition of effective and efficient learning strategies?

- Does the administration provide the resources to support and foster the use of a variety of curricular options and instructional strategies?

ACCOUNTABILITY AND EVALUATION

One assumption of the school reform movement is that greater accountability can be achieved by systematically supervising and monitoring the performance of all students. There is a danger that as schools are held accountable for higher academic standards, inappropriate emphasis will be given to the results of such measures as national achievement tests or "report cards." Reliance on such measures may not permit evaluation of program effectiveness for students with learning disabilities.

Questions to Consider

- Are the design and content of tests and the testing process appropriate to measure the educational progress of students with learning disabilities?

- What broader assessment systems can be used to evaluate the progress of students with learning disabilities and therefore to serve as additional indices of school accountability?

SCHOOL AND CLASSROOM ORGANIZATION

Organizational designs that stem from school reform efforts do not necessarily address federal requirements (i.e., P.L. 94-142) for providing a full continuum of specialized and related services. For example, although consultation and collaboration are effective approaches for enhancing services to students with learning disabilities, there is a danger that they will be used as substitutes for a full continuum of educational placement options.

Grouping students by ability and increasing the time students spend in school without providing appropriate academic supports will not enhance excellence or equity for students with learning disabilities. Teachers must be encouraged to use a variety of effective grouping strategies; otherwise, students with learning disabilities may assume passive roles in groups or may be unable to participate in appropriate ways. Students with learning disabilities may not benefit from extended school programs unless individualized approaches and modifications are offered.

Questions to Consider

- Are the needs of students with learning disabilities considered in decisions about grouping?

- Are different groupings used to address different instructional goals?

- Are regular and special education teachers, related service personnel, parents, and students involved in school building decisions about grouping?

- Are communities aware of the full implications of extending the length of school programs?

- Do the design and implementation of service delivery options reflect an understanding of what learning disabilities are and what implications they have for appropriate services?

- Does the administration promote and support a variety of service delivery options?

- Is time provided for collaborative planning?

LOCUS OF DECISION MAKING

School reform proposals often include recommendations for a shift in the locus of decision making. Several concerns emerge in connection with such strategies as school-based management, teacher empowerment, and increased parent involvement. Potential exists for inequity in programs and services from building to building. The expertise that is needed for ongoing program development and evaluation, as well as teacher supervision and evaluation, may not exist at the school level. Some building-level administrators are unfamiliar either with the needs of individuals with learning disabilities or with ways of meeting these needs. Similarly, some regular classroom teachers may not know what the needs of individuals with learning disabilities are and how to manage diversity within the classroom.

Special education and related service personnel and community members with disabilities (consumers) may not be included in the decision-making process at the building level. In addition, schools may involve parents at a superficial level yet not include them in the actual decision-making process. Even given the opportunity to share in decision making, parents, school personnel, and community members may not have the skills they need for full participation.

Questions to Consider

- Do parents, professional personnel, and community members have a meaningful role in local decision-making processes?

- How do schools prepare parents and community members to participate as partners in the decision-making process?

- Are individuals with disabilities involved in the local decision-making processes?

- Are programs, services, resources, and curricular opportunities equitable among local schools?

- Do school personnel have the expertise to make decisions about educational needs of individuals with learning disabilities?

- Does each school have adequate program supervision and evaluation?

- Are special education and related service personnel involved in developing accountability systems, designing programs and services, and participating in other activities at the local level?

CHOICE

The concept of parental choice is intended to allow parents to choose the school that their children will attend. It is often assumed that parental choice will stimulate excellence in educational practice. However, parental choice may have unforeseen consequences for students with learning disabilities in that they may be neglected and placed in weakened and underfunded public schools.

Questions to Consider

- What educational opportunities are available to students with learning disabilities under a choice-driven system?

- What constraints will students experience because of their unique needs?

- Will nonpublic schools be obligated to provide appropriate individualized educational services for students with learning disabilities?

- Who will monitor the consequences and influences of choice-driven systems on students with learning disabilities?

- Will added costs for transportation and administration prevent or interfere with choices for students?

SCHOOL FINANCES

School reform and school finances are inextricably related. Thus, national determination of school reform must be coupled with a careful evaluation of educational funding. The lack of consistency in efforts to improve education can be understood, in part, as being directly related to variations in federal and state supports and provisions.

Whatever financial system is used in educational funding, it must provide for the equitable education of students with learning disabilities. For example, voucher systems must ensure that necessary funds and resources will be available for students with learning disabilities. Similarly, when local schools are responsible for total financial management, equity in fund allocation must be ensured for these students.

Questions to Consider

- How will the school reform movement influence the availability of funds for students with special needs?

- With a decrease in available general revenue, will dollars be used for regular education to the exclusion of special education?

- If equal amounts of money are allocated per student, are all students served equitably?

- How will equity be ensured in the application of new school finance procedures?

- How will block grants influence the availability of funds for students with special needs?

- If regular and special education dollars are commingled, how will services to students with special needs be affected?

- Is the placement of students in regular education a device to reduce spending for special education, or is it in the best interests of children?

PERSONNEL PREPARATION

Well-prepared administrators, teachers, and related service personnel are fundamental to school improvement. The competencies they need include sufficient depth of knowledge in the content areas, ability to meet the diverse needs of a wide range of students, and thorough appreciation of teaching and classroom management strategies. If personnel preparation programs focus only on content mastery, the result will be personnel who are not prepared to work collaboratively or provide appropriate individualized instruction for students using a variety of service delivery systems.

School reform may result in students with learning disabilities being placed in the regular classroom for the entire school day. If so, administrators, teachers, and related service personnel must be trained to meet these students' specific educational needs. Therefore, effective school reform must include provisions to enable practicing teachers and other personnel to renew and refine their professional skills as needed.

Questions to Consider

- How do reform initiatives address preservice and inservice preparation programs for school personnel?

- How are professionals prepared to understand the nature of learning disabilities and the manner in which different disabilities affect how individuals learn?

- To what extent do personnel preparation programs prepare teachers, administrators, and related service personnel to provide accommodations for students with special needs in the regular classroom?

- To what extent are school personnel prepared and able to use different instructional approaches that meet the individual needs of students with learning disabilities?

- How are related service personnel trained to fulfill their changing roles in educational settings?
- Do institutions of higher education maintain effective criteria for personnel preparation programs?
- Are practica and field experiences interdisciplinary in nature, and are they designed to promote collaboration?
- Are needs assessment data used to develop inservice programs?
- How is an interdisciplinary, collaborative perspective maintained in the design and implementation of service programs?

CONCLUSION

The school reform movement may adversely affect students with learning disabilities unless parents and professionals respond to its initiatives. These students may be ignored, and their needs unacknowledged, as the initiatives of the reform movement are planned and implemented. As a consequence, these students will become part of a larger group of students who are taught without regard for their individual needs.

Therefore, educators and parents cannot ignore the reform movement; in fact, they must provide leadership at national, state, and local levels. This report demonstrates NJCLD's deep concern and desire that parents, professionals and policy makers work cooperatively in planning and implementing reforms. We strongly urge that strategies be developed within the reform movement to improve education for students with learning disabilities.

REFERENCES

Education for All Handicapped Children Act of 1975, 20 U.S.C. § 1400 *et seq.*
Goals 2000: Educate America Act, 20 U.S.C. § 5801 *et seq.*